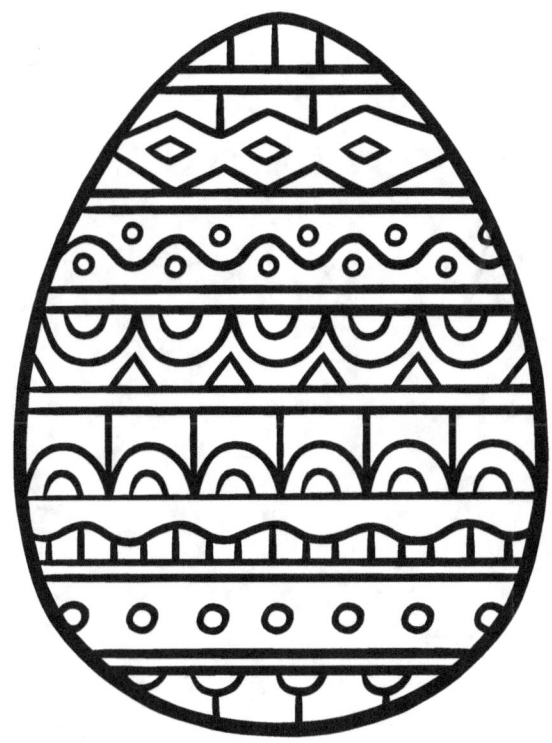
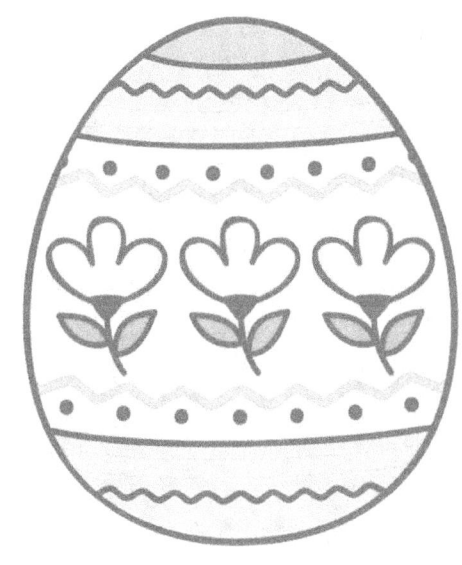

Copyright © 2022
Published by
Amanzi Books

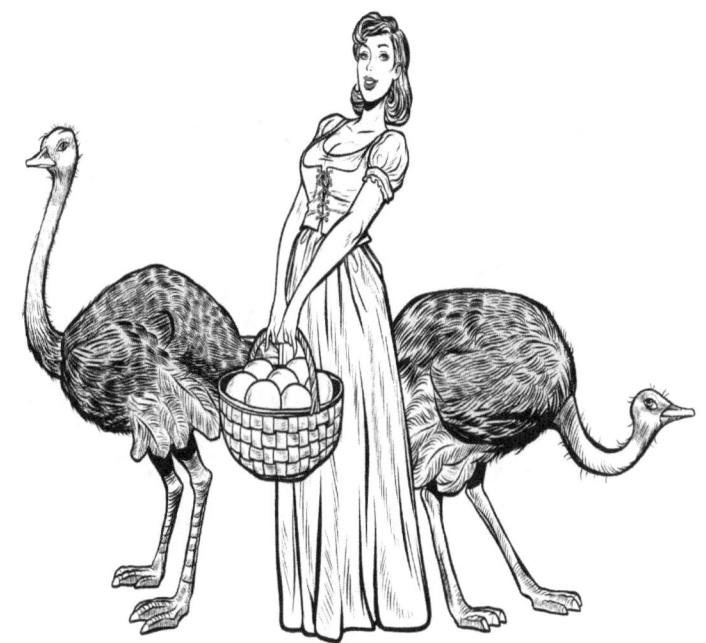

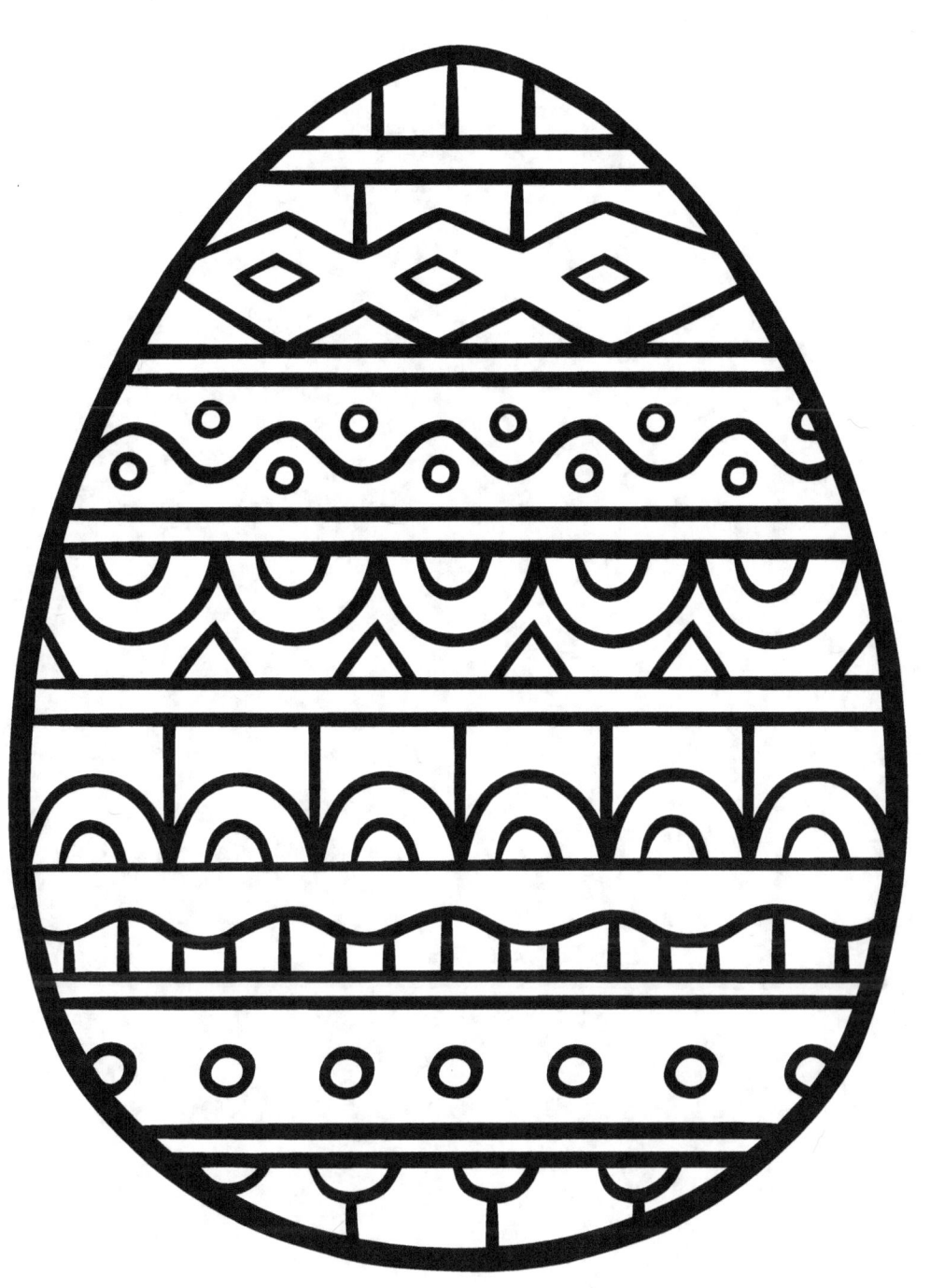

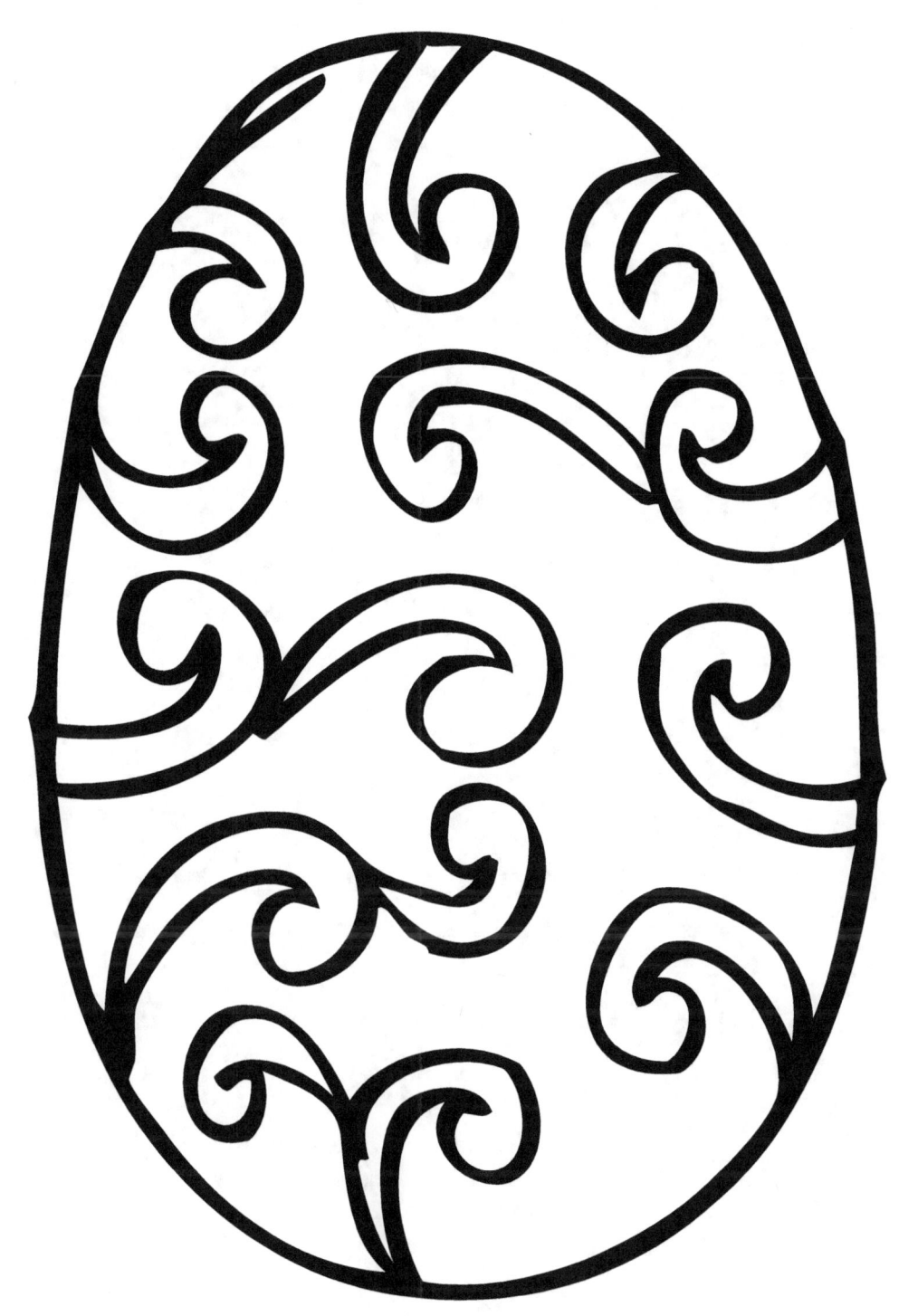

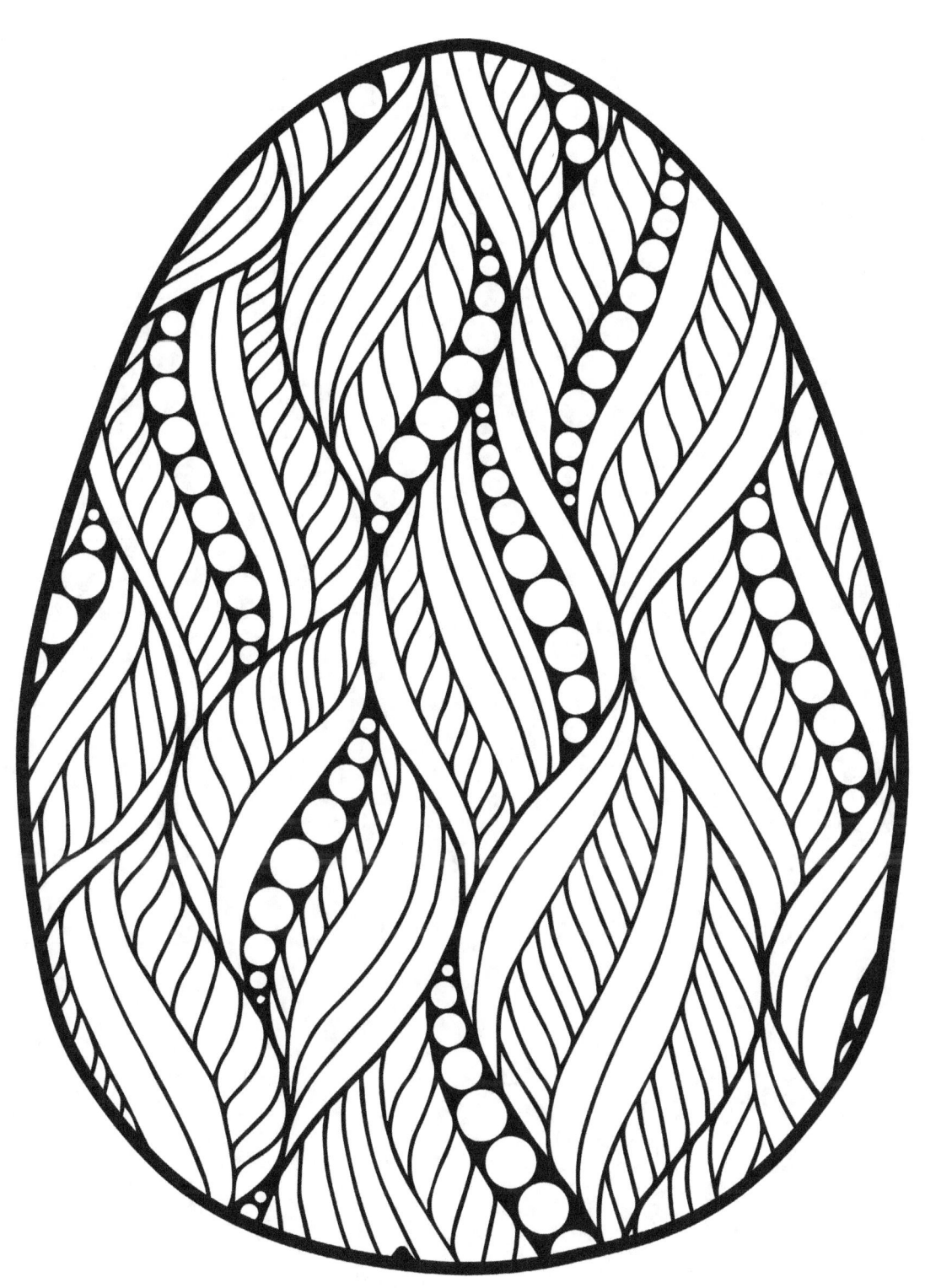

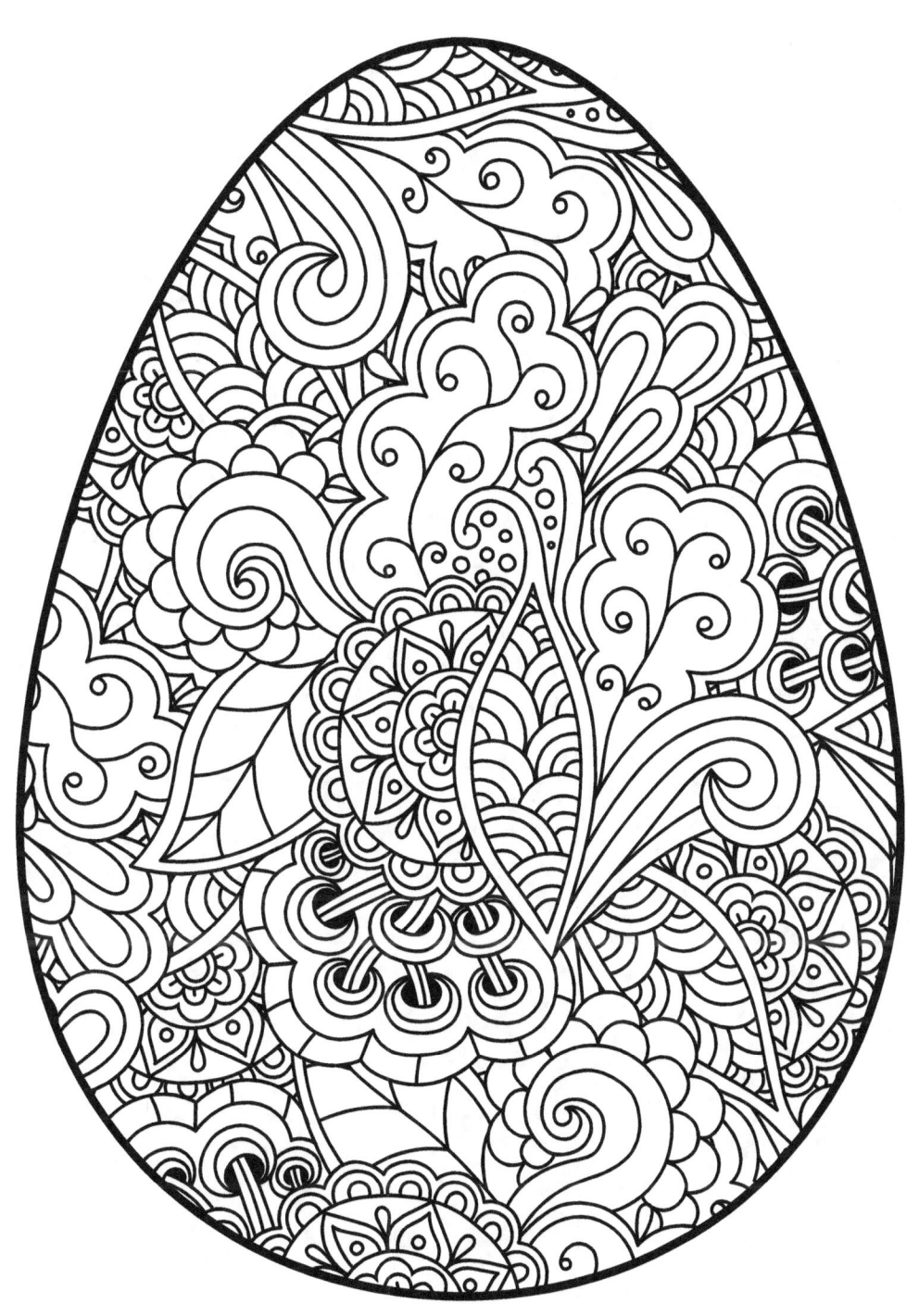

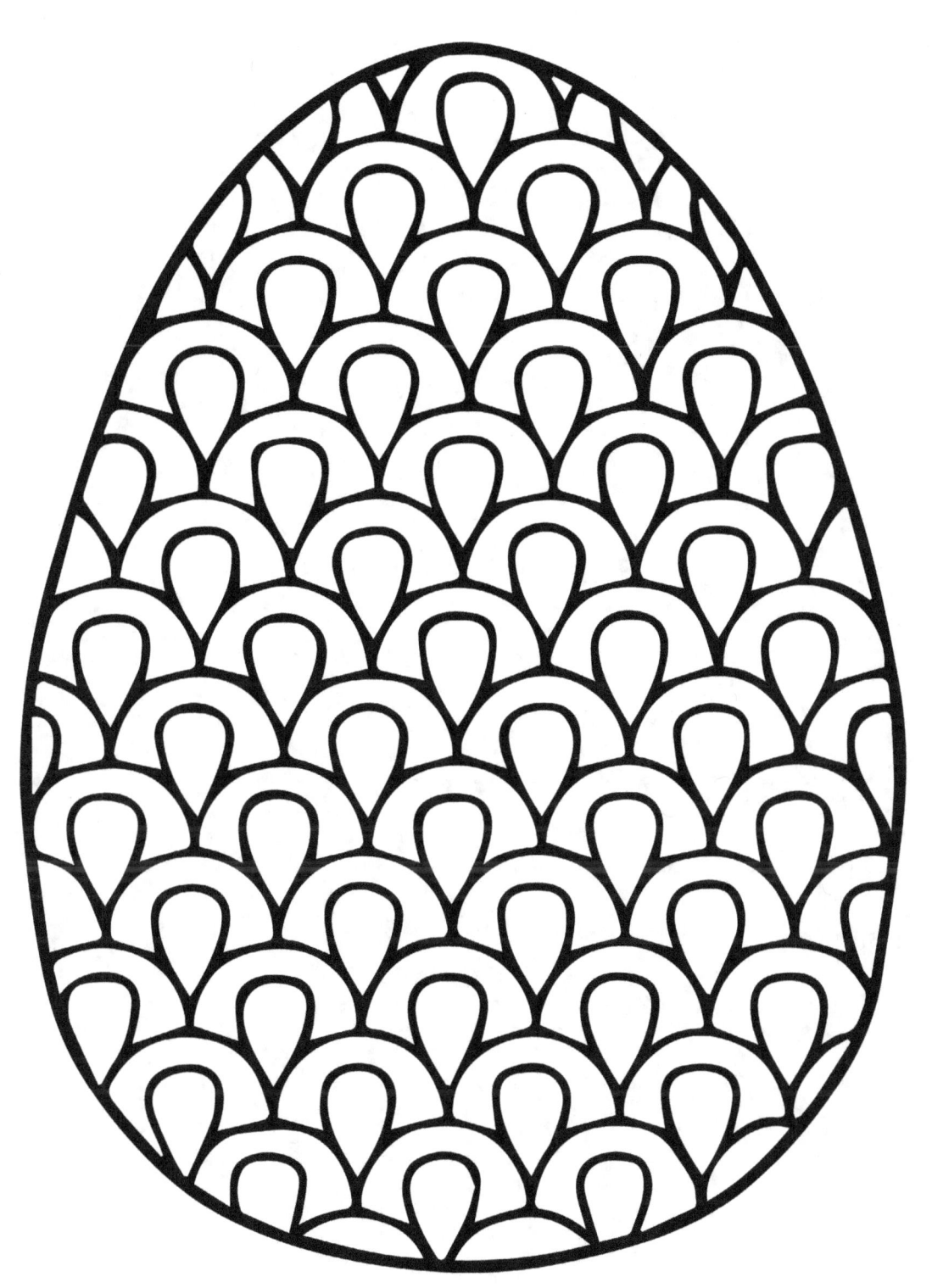

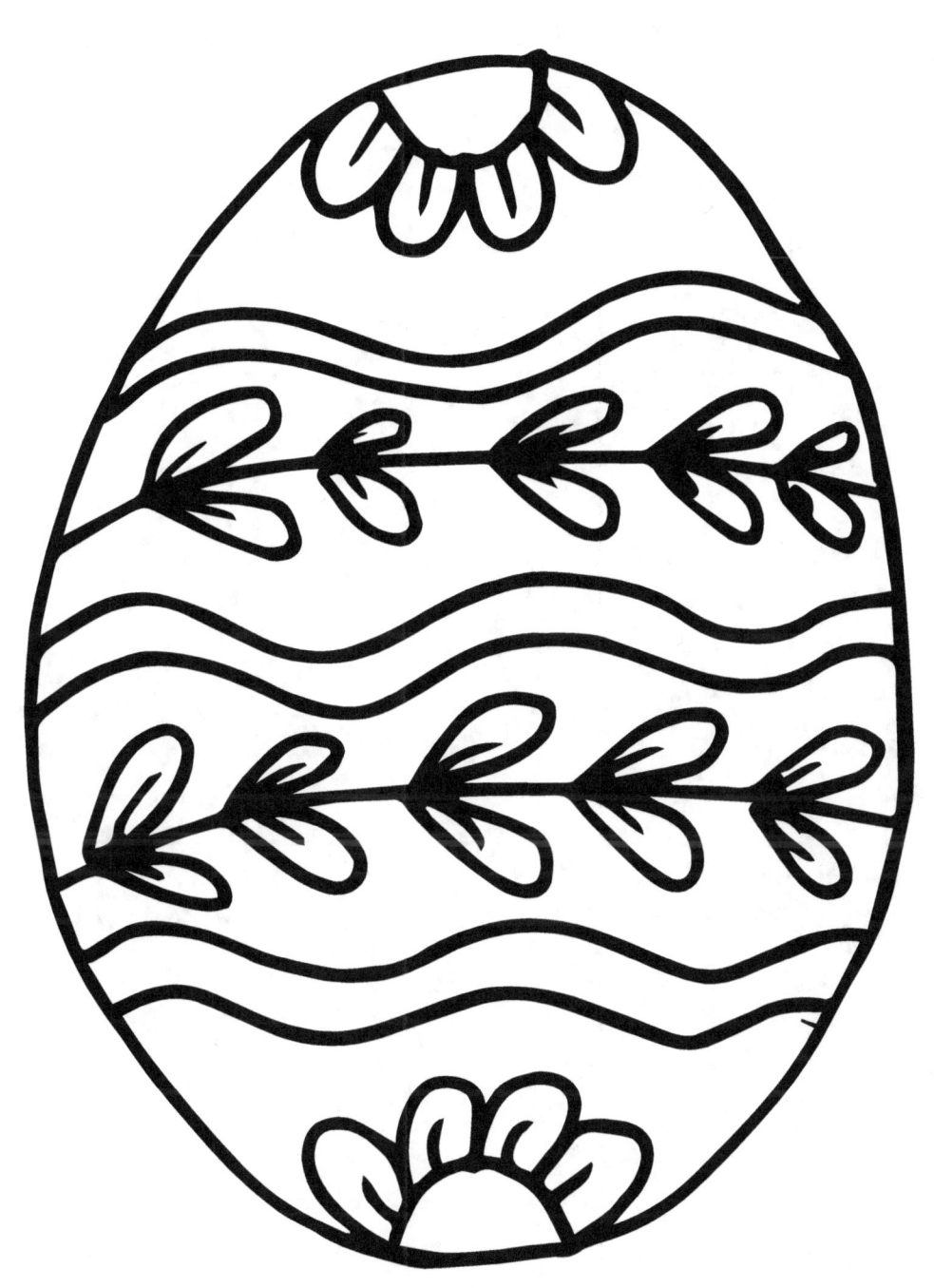

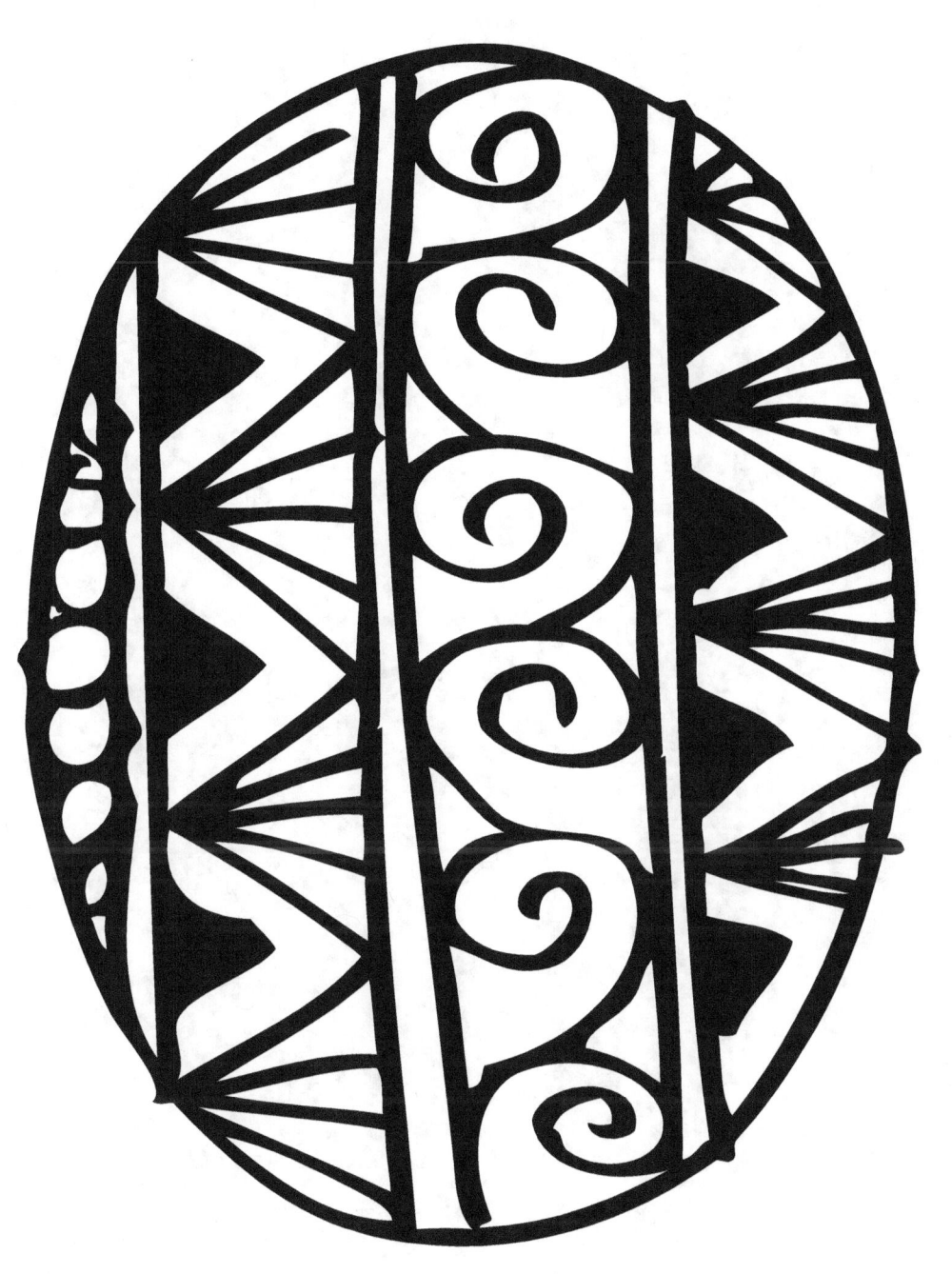

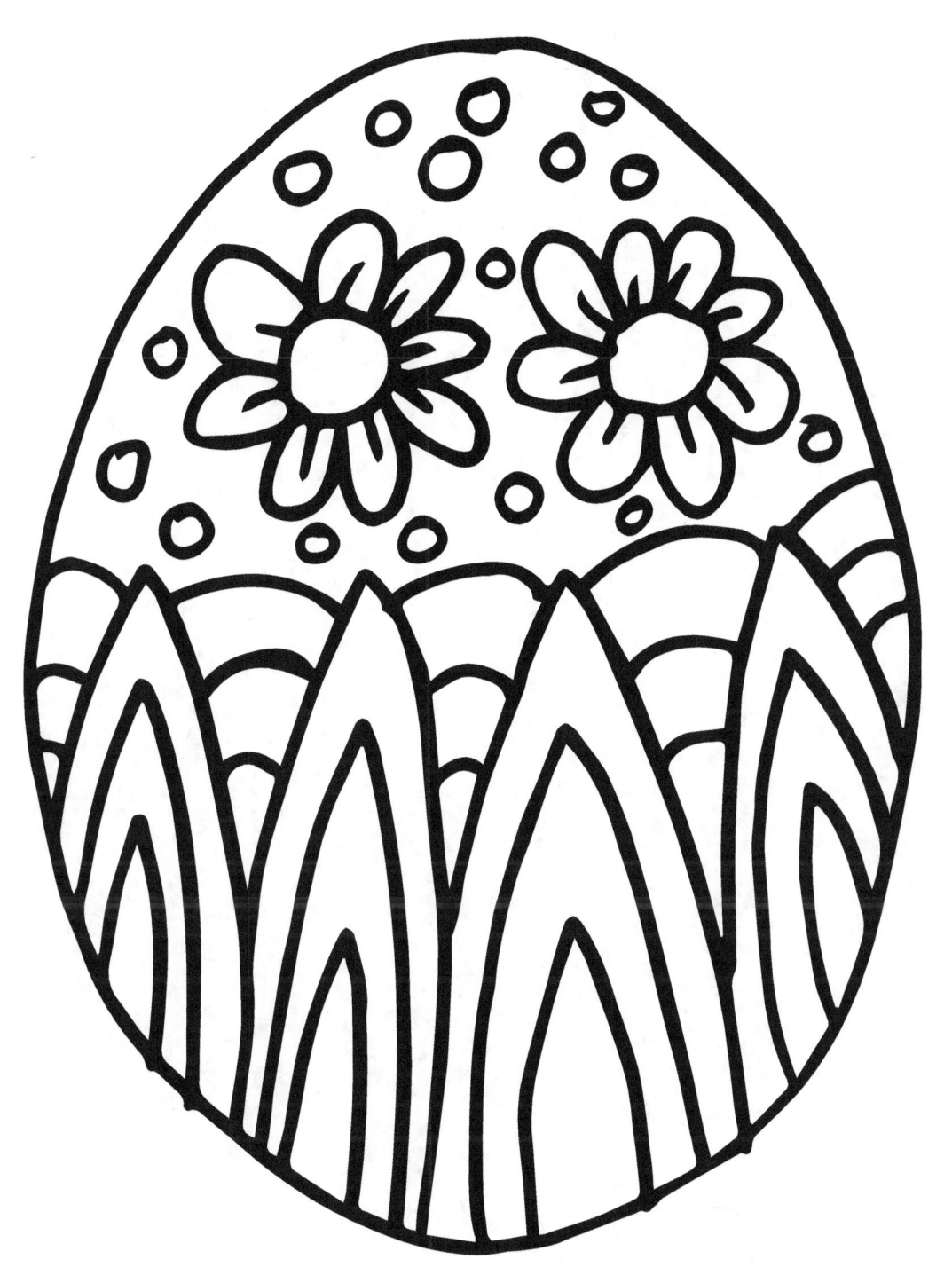

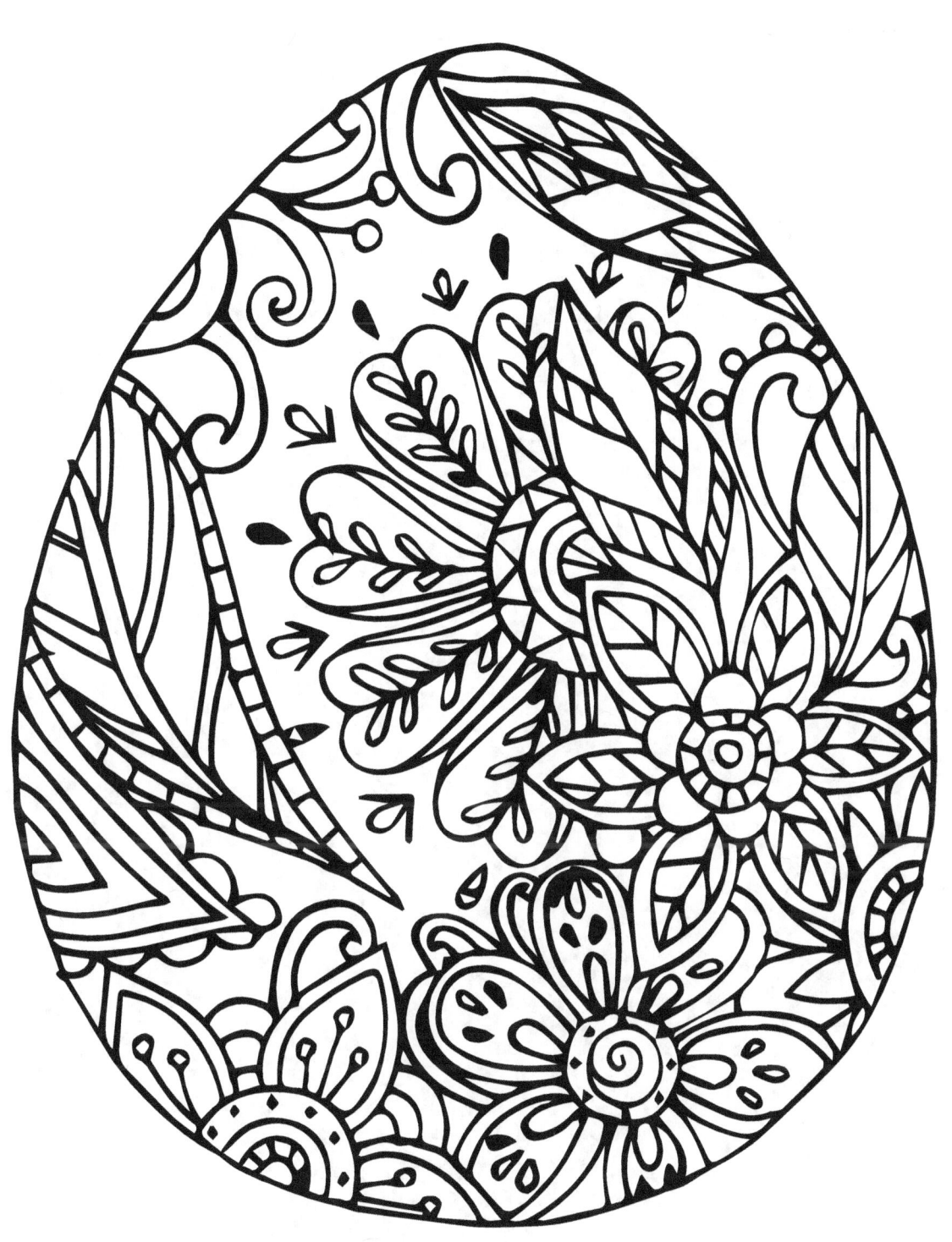

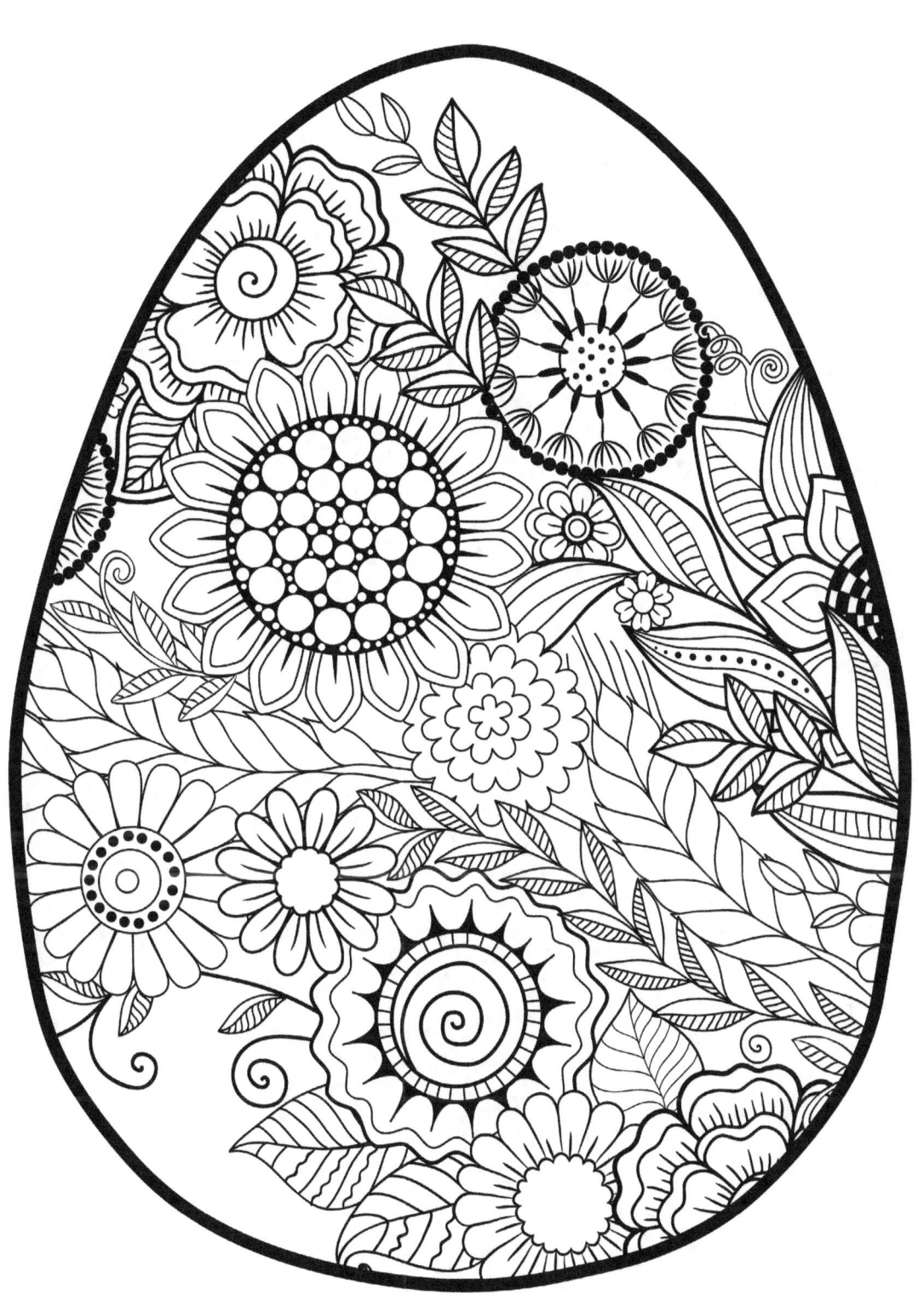

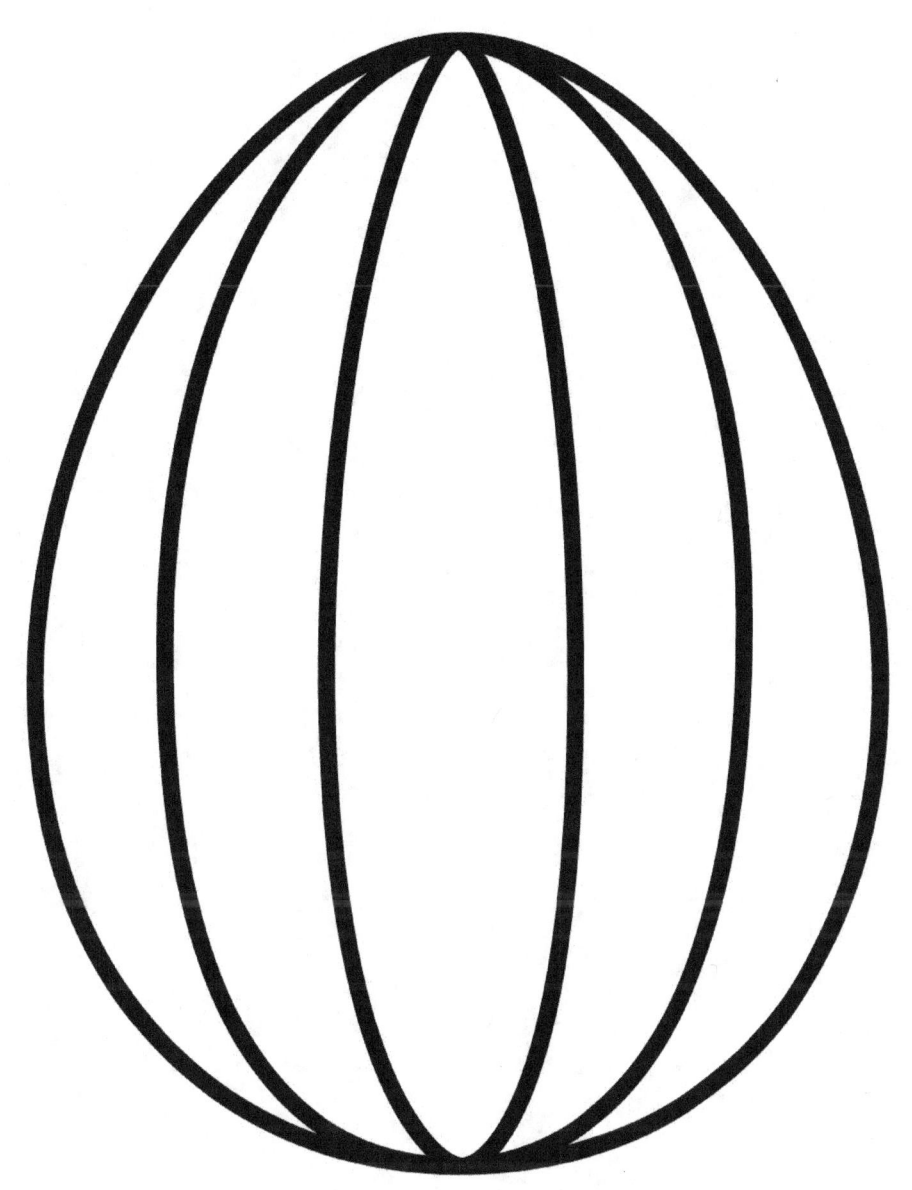

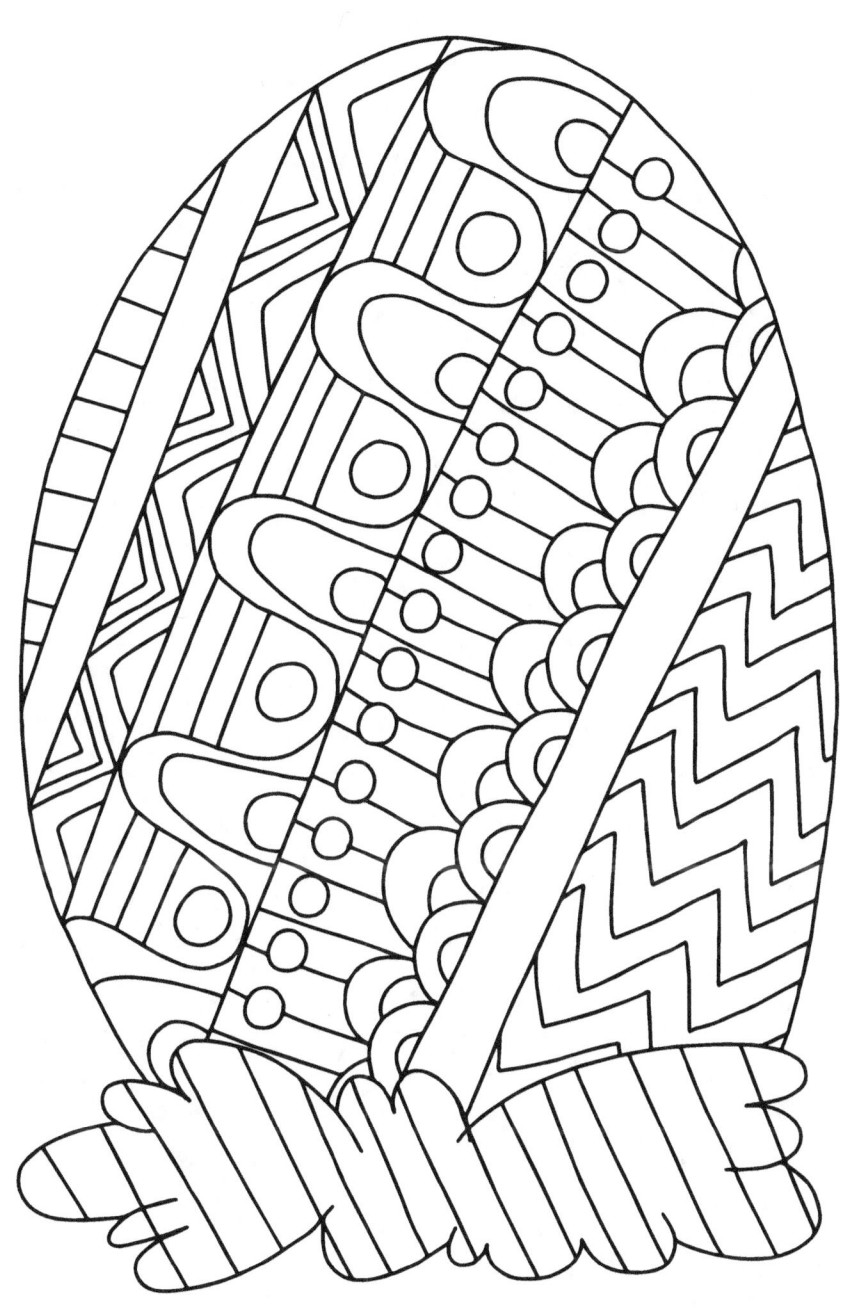

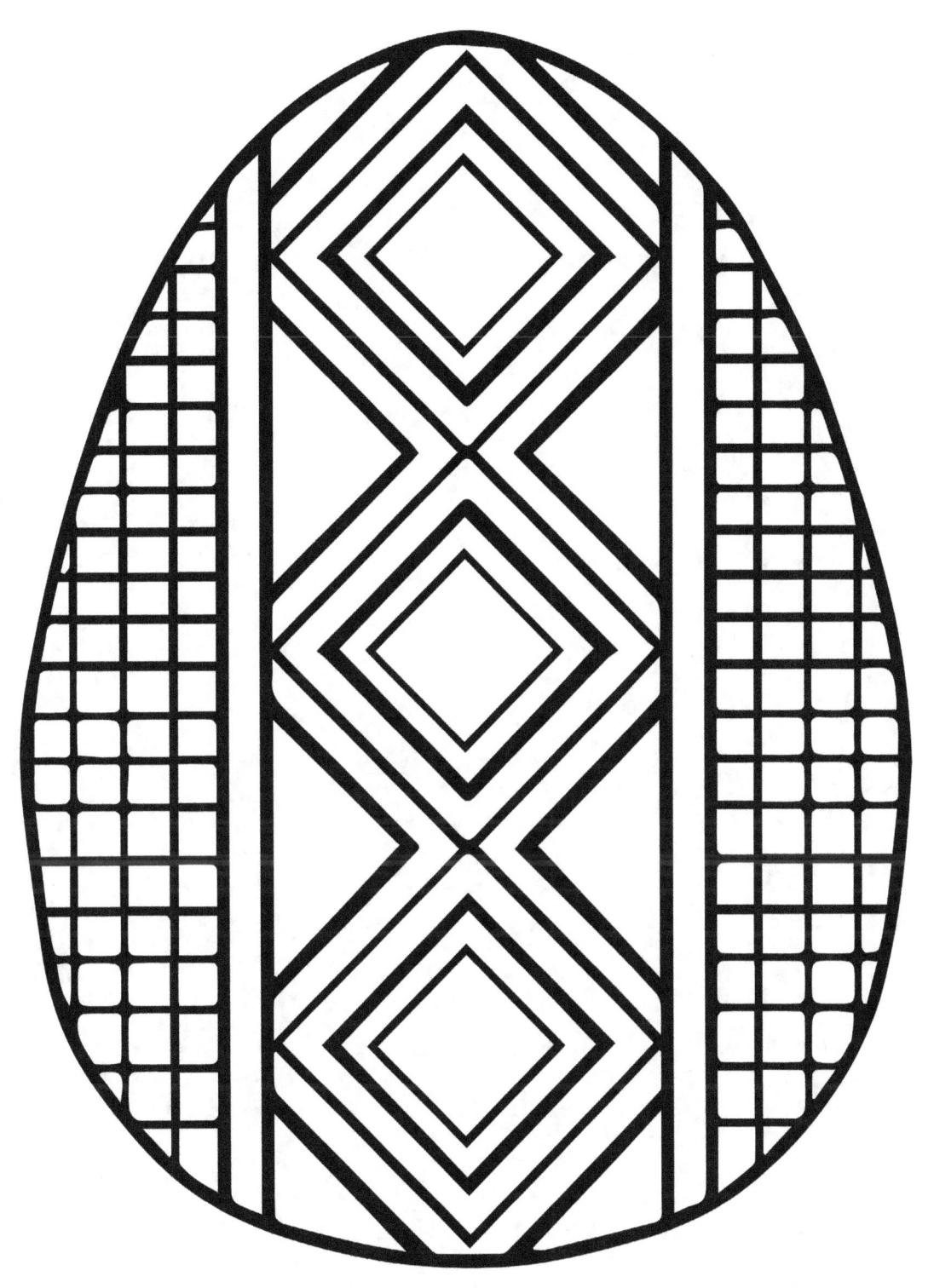

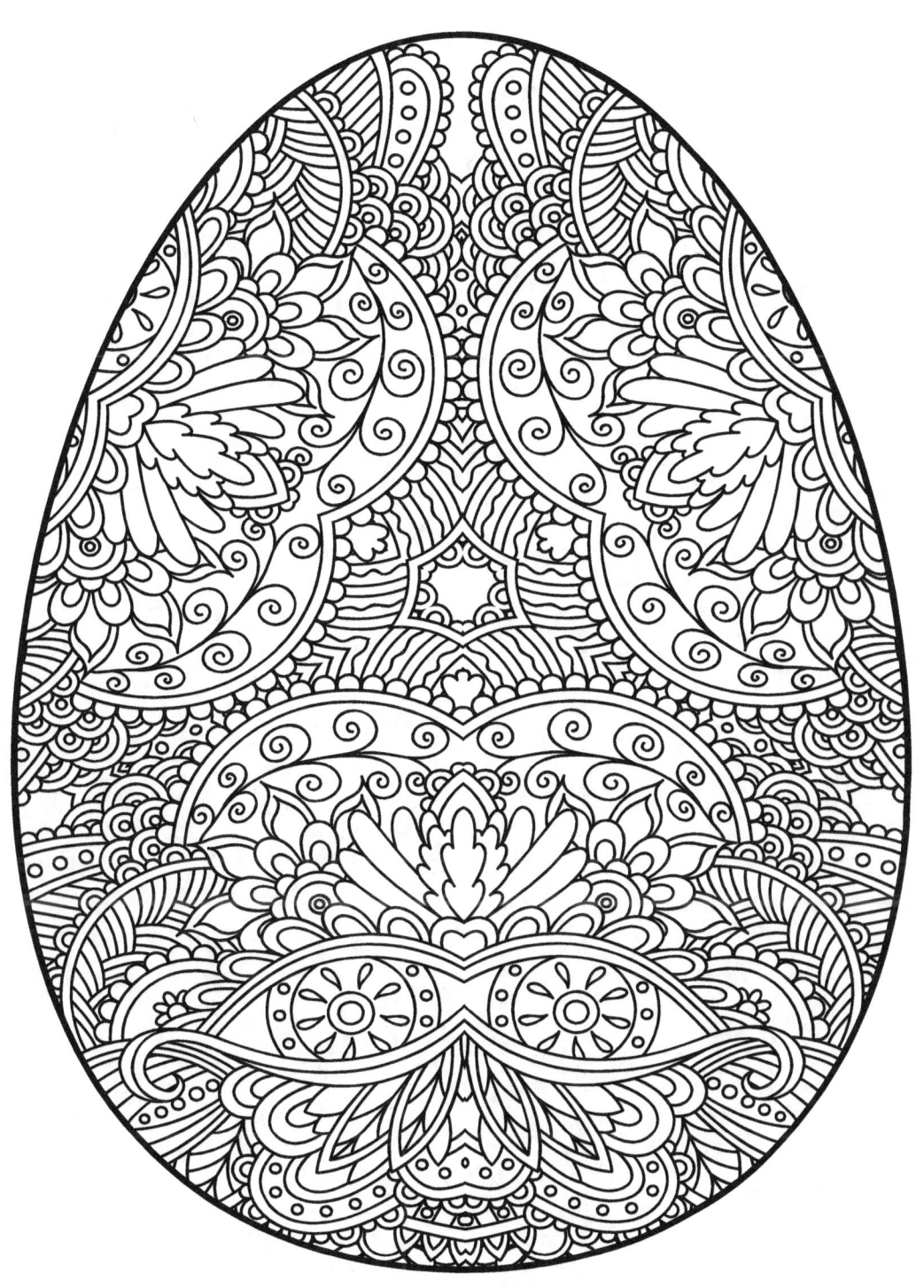

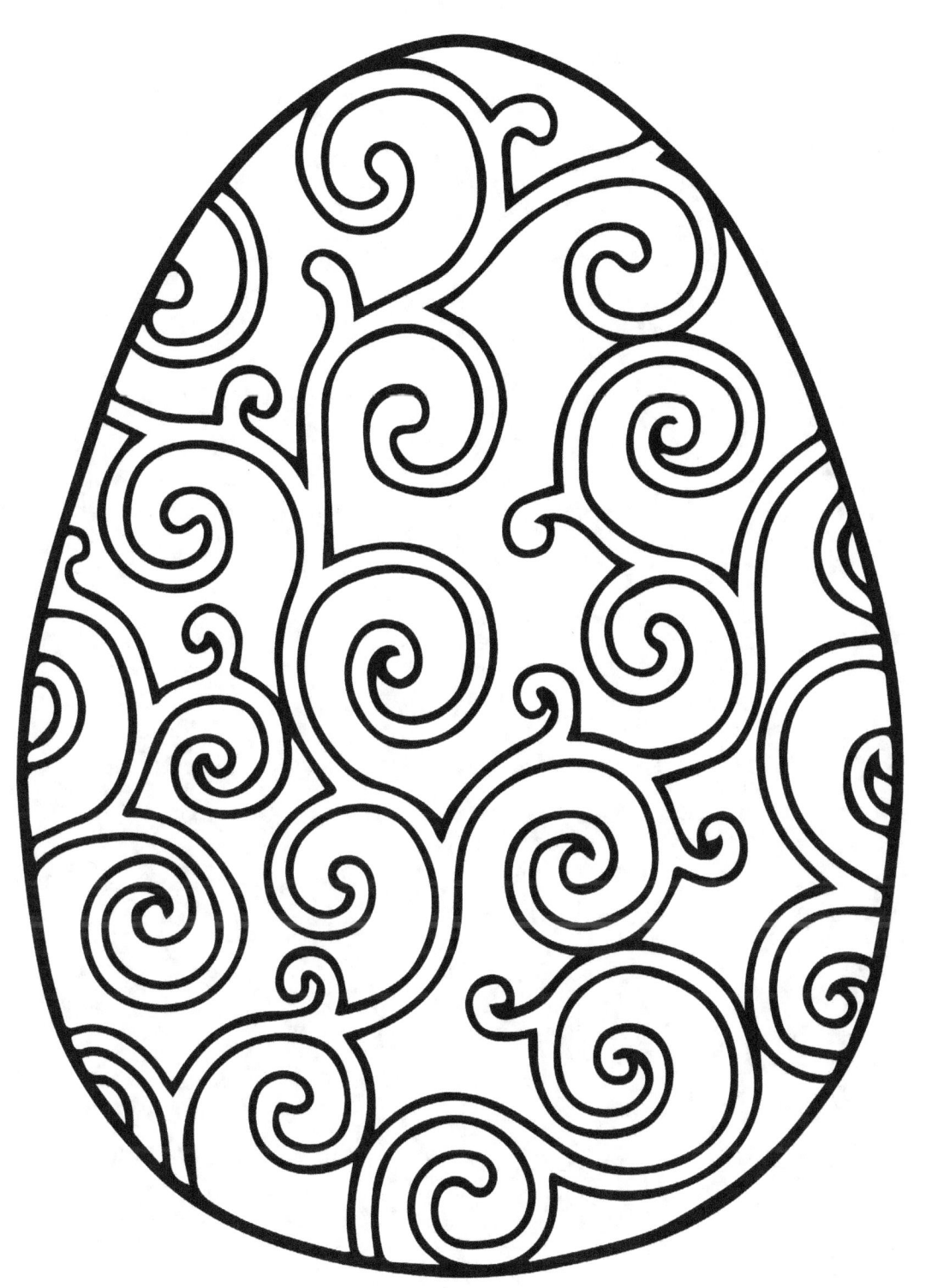

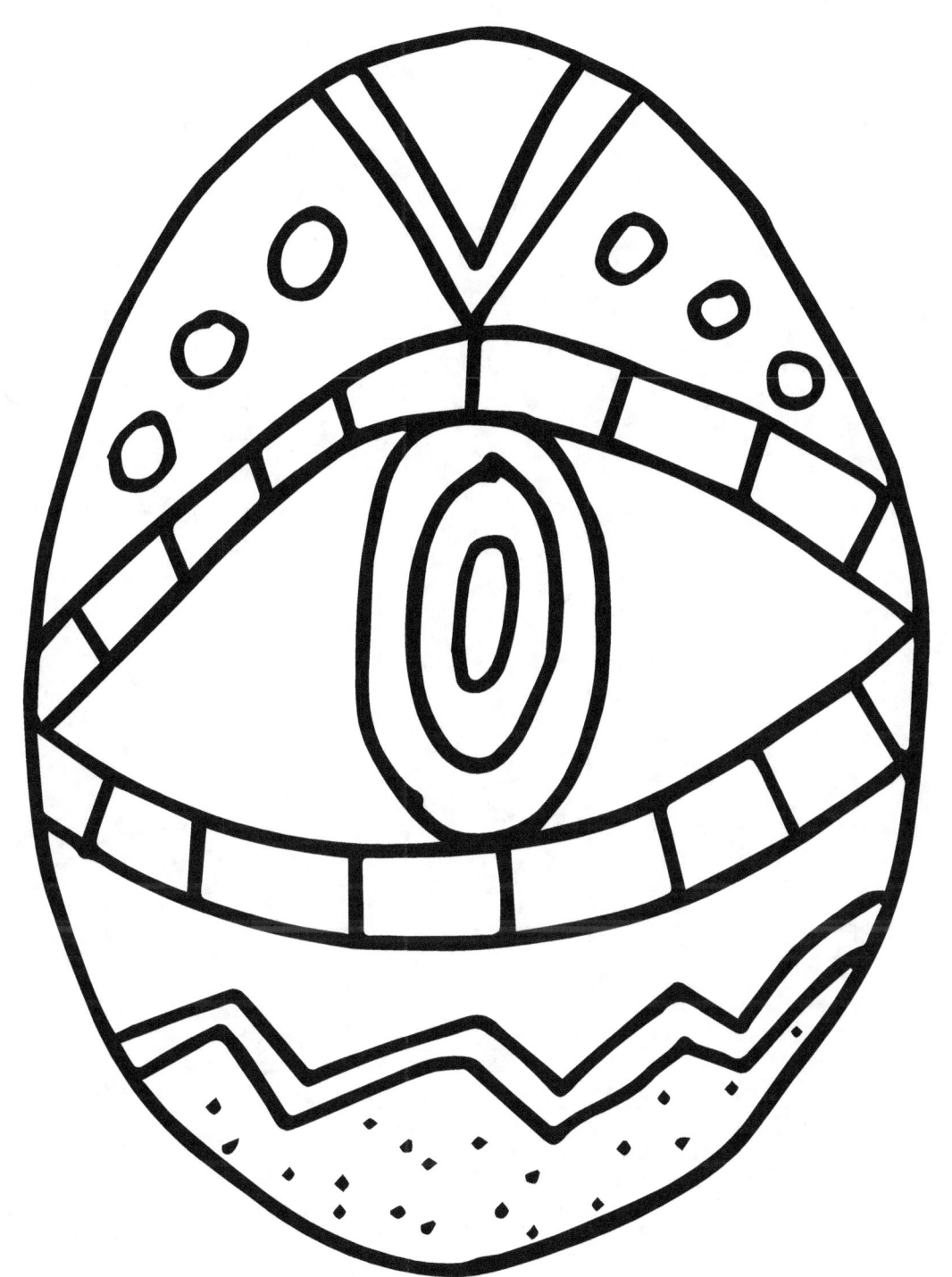

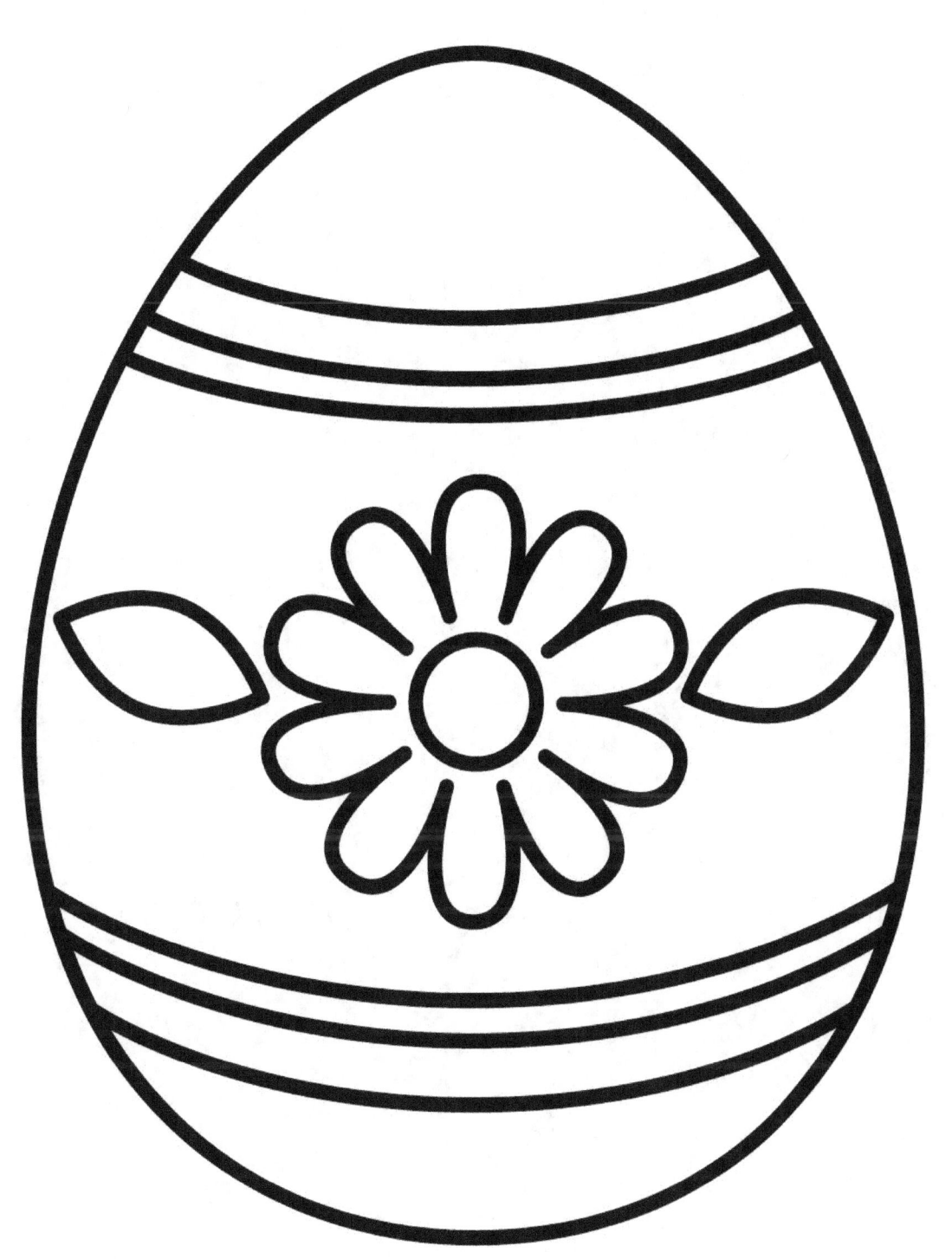

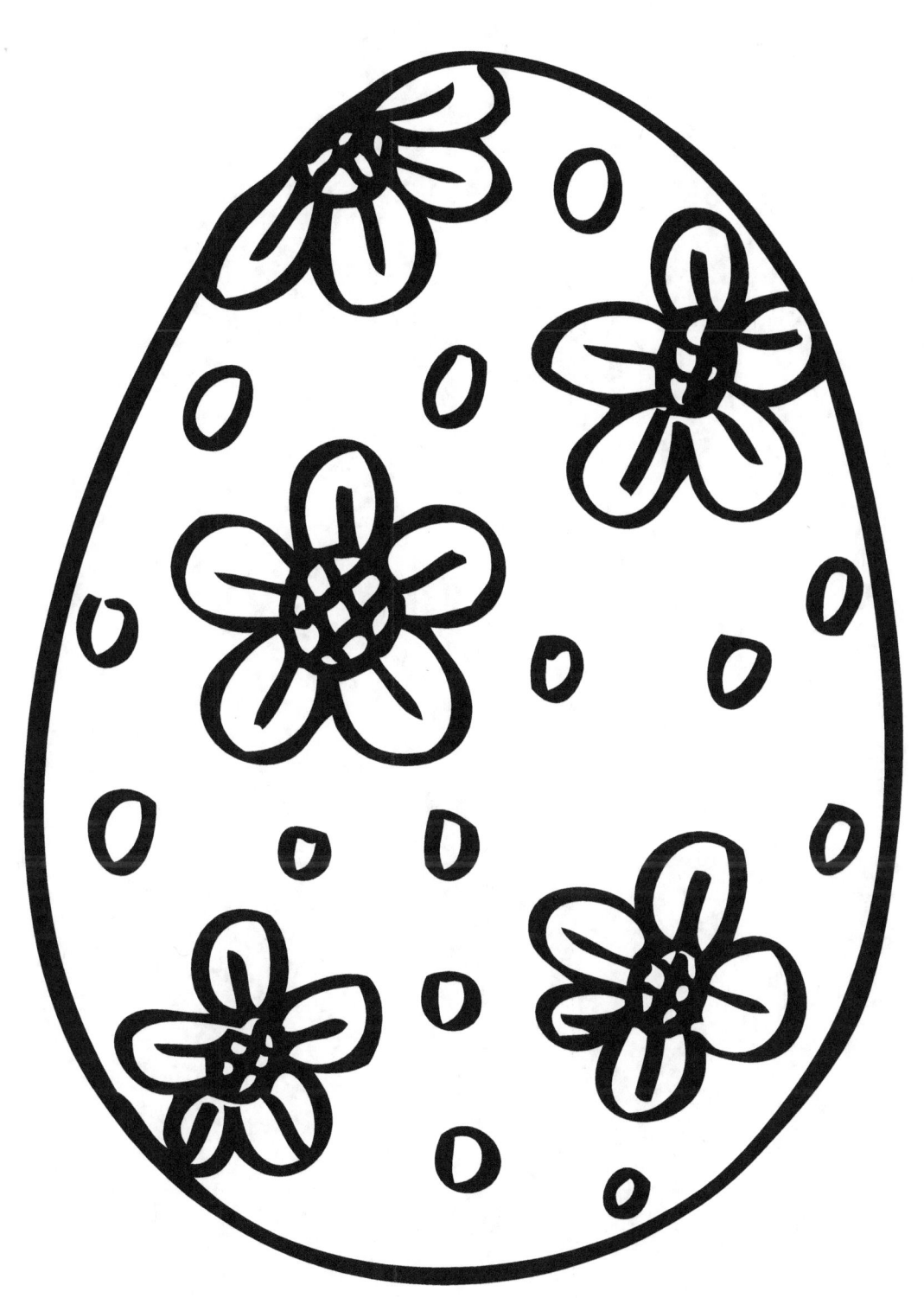

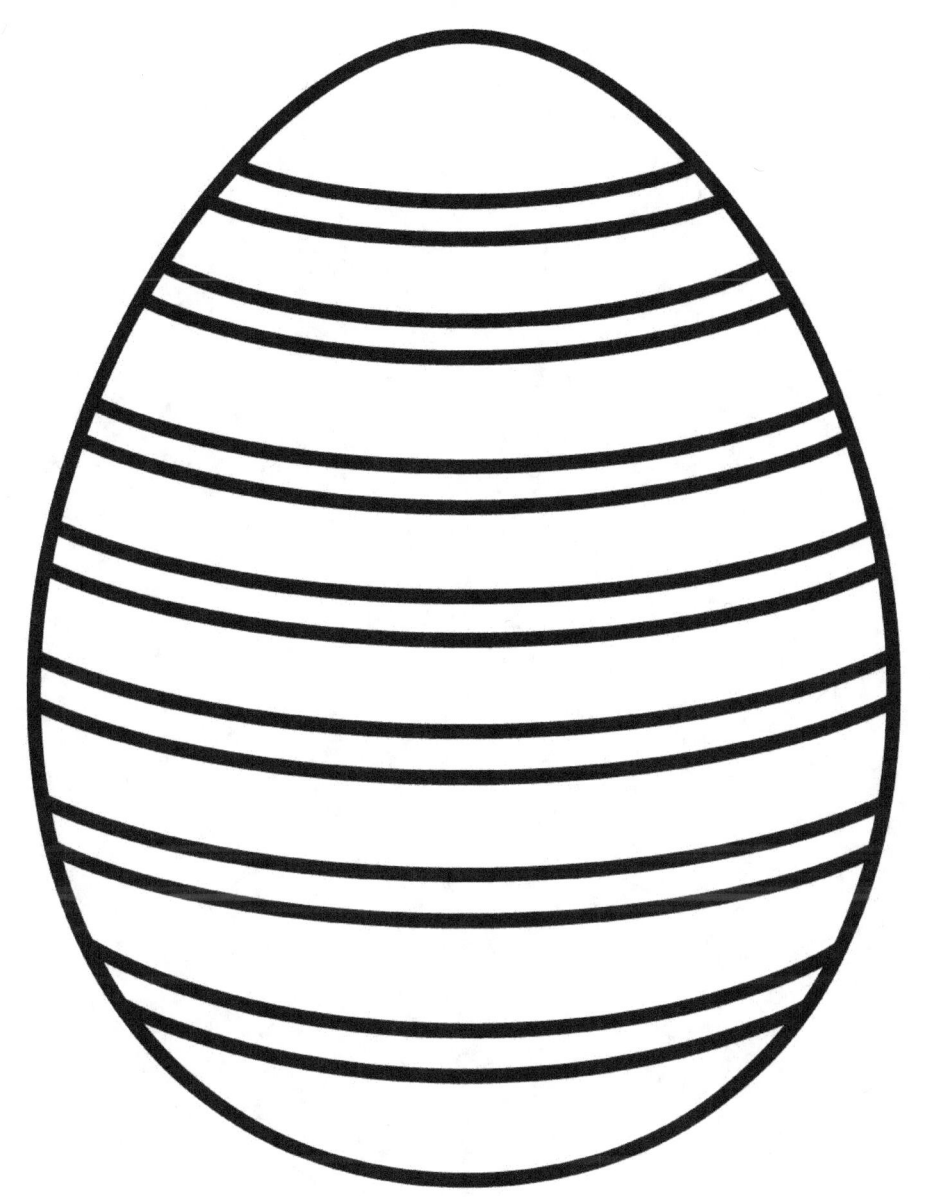

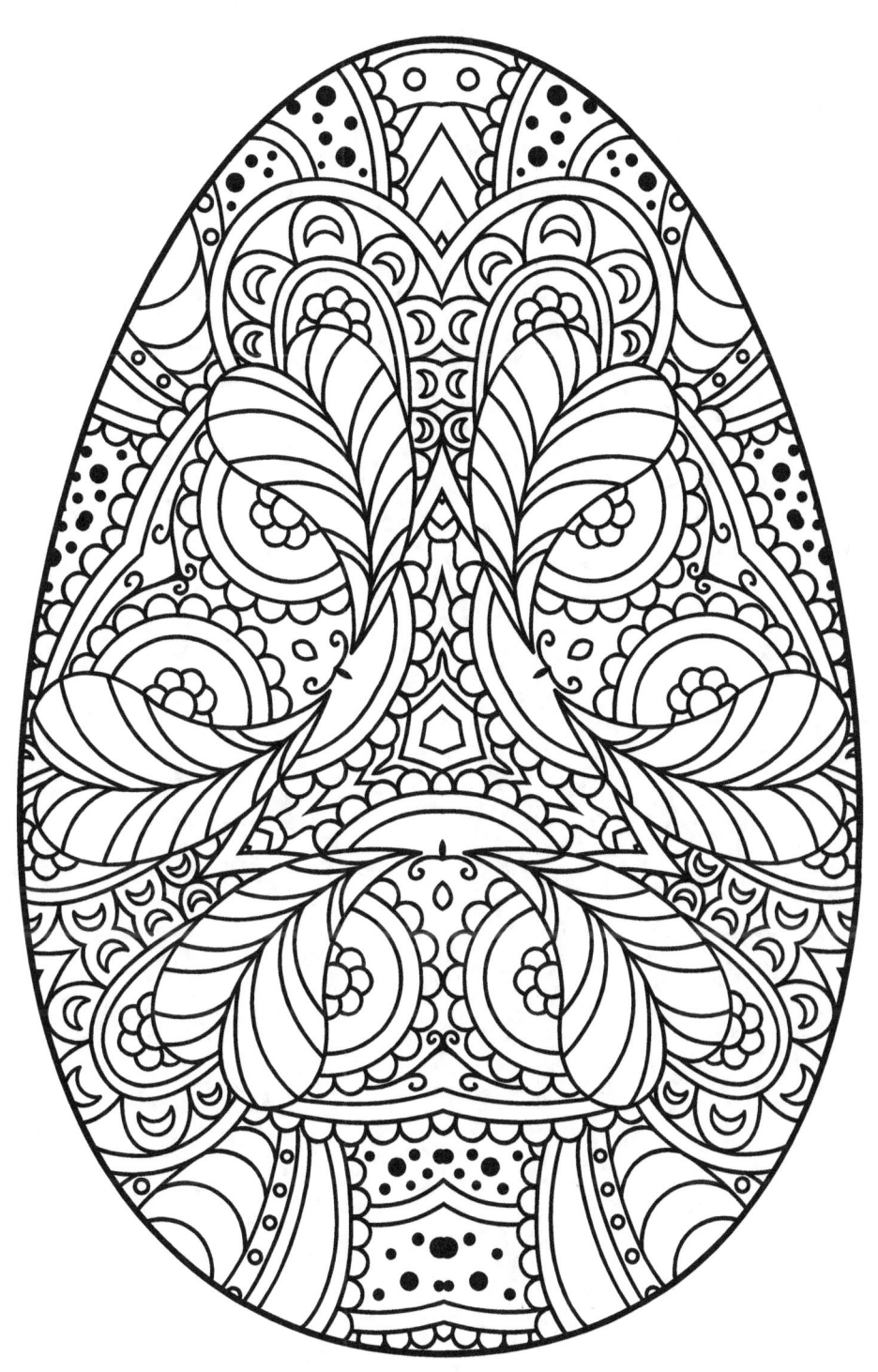

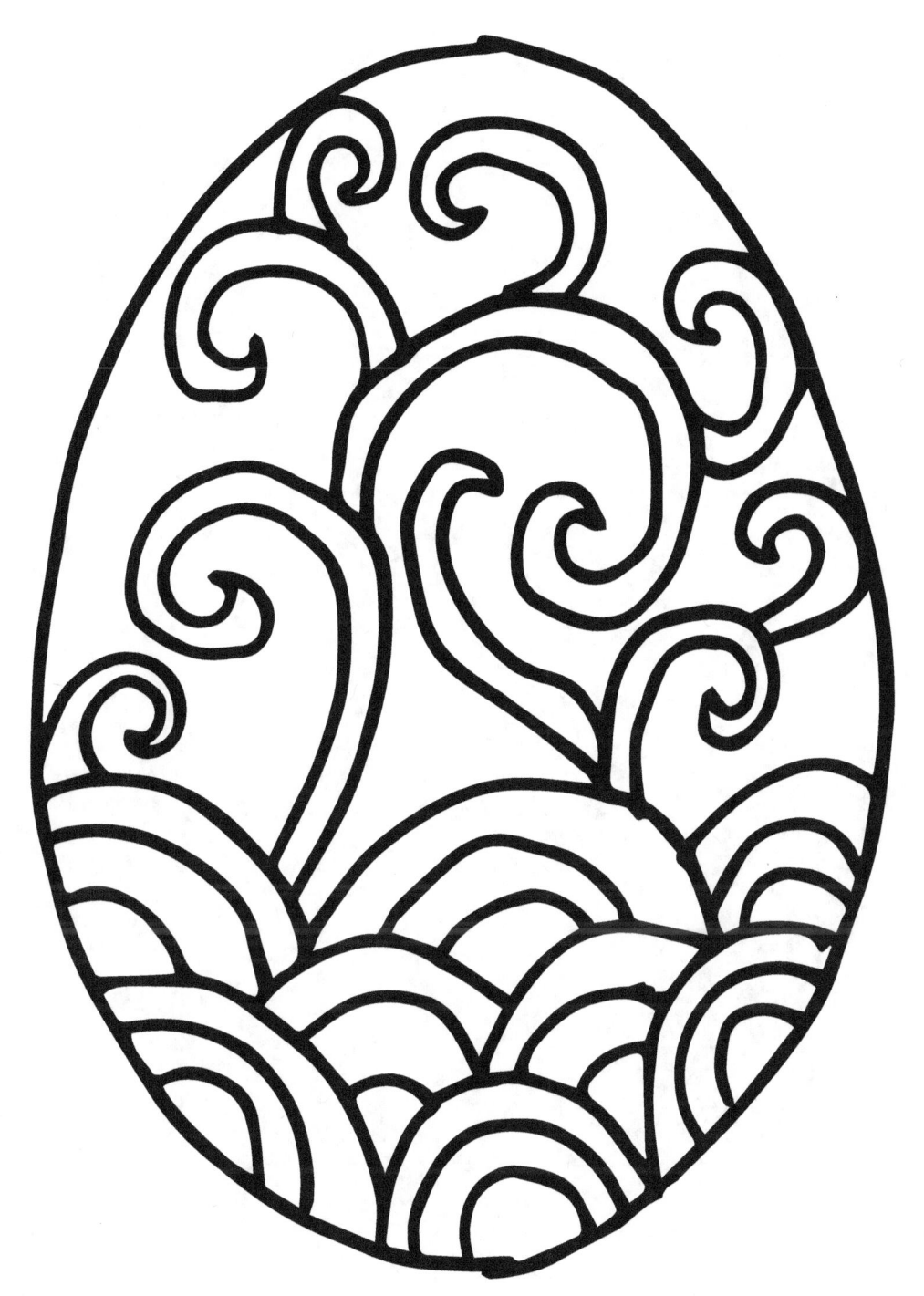

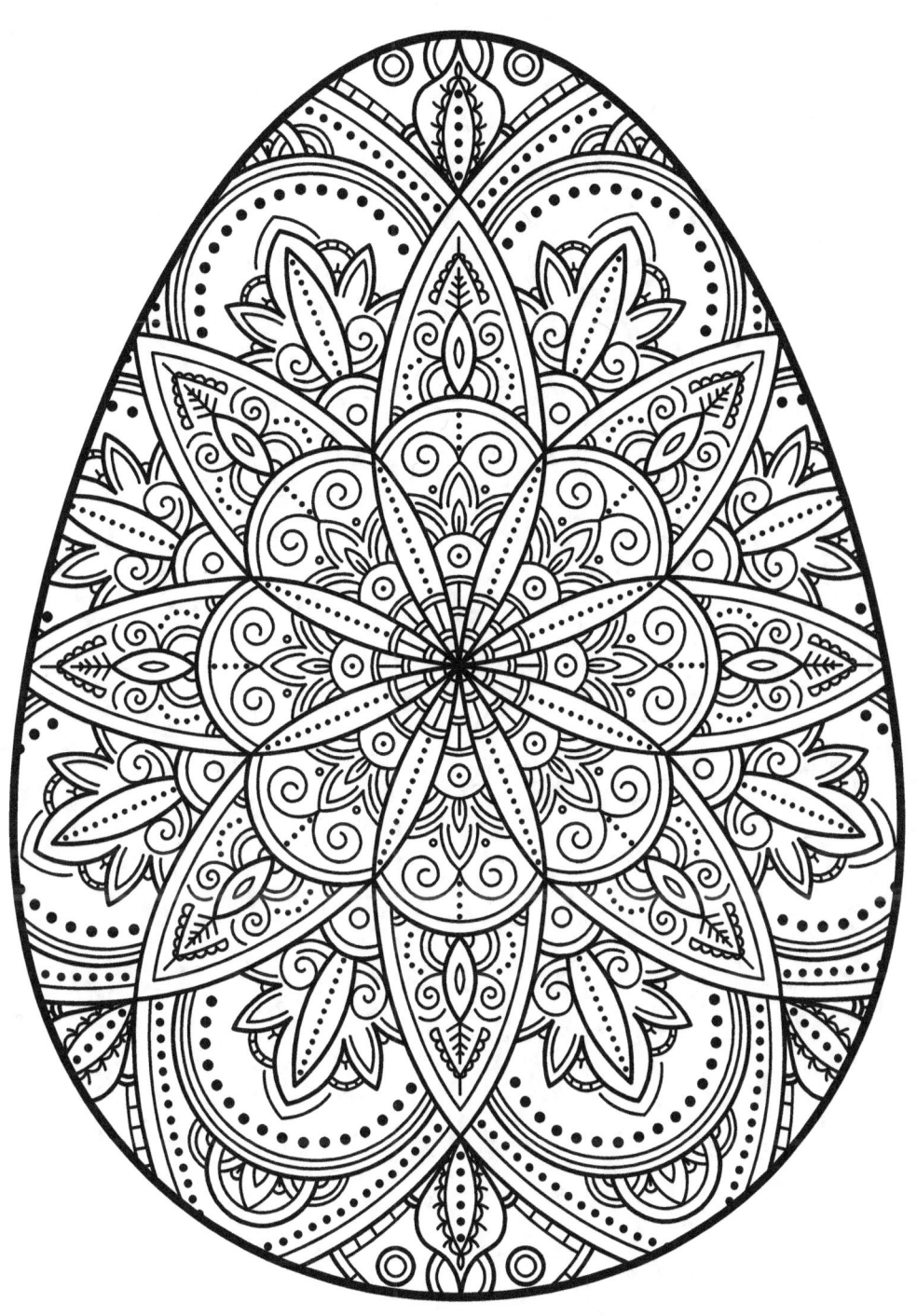

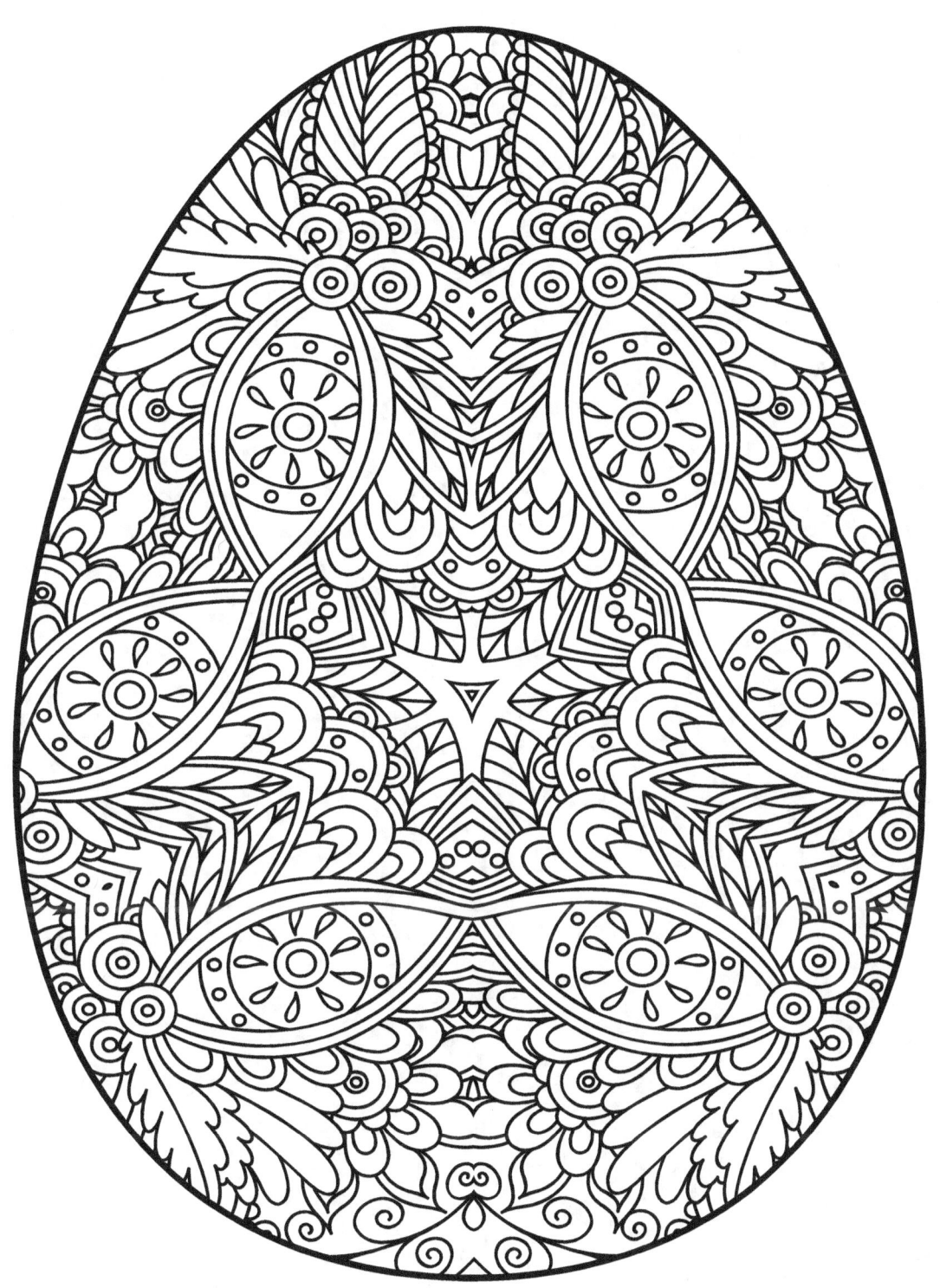

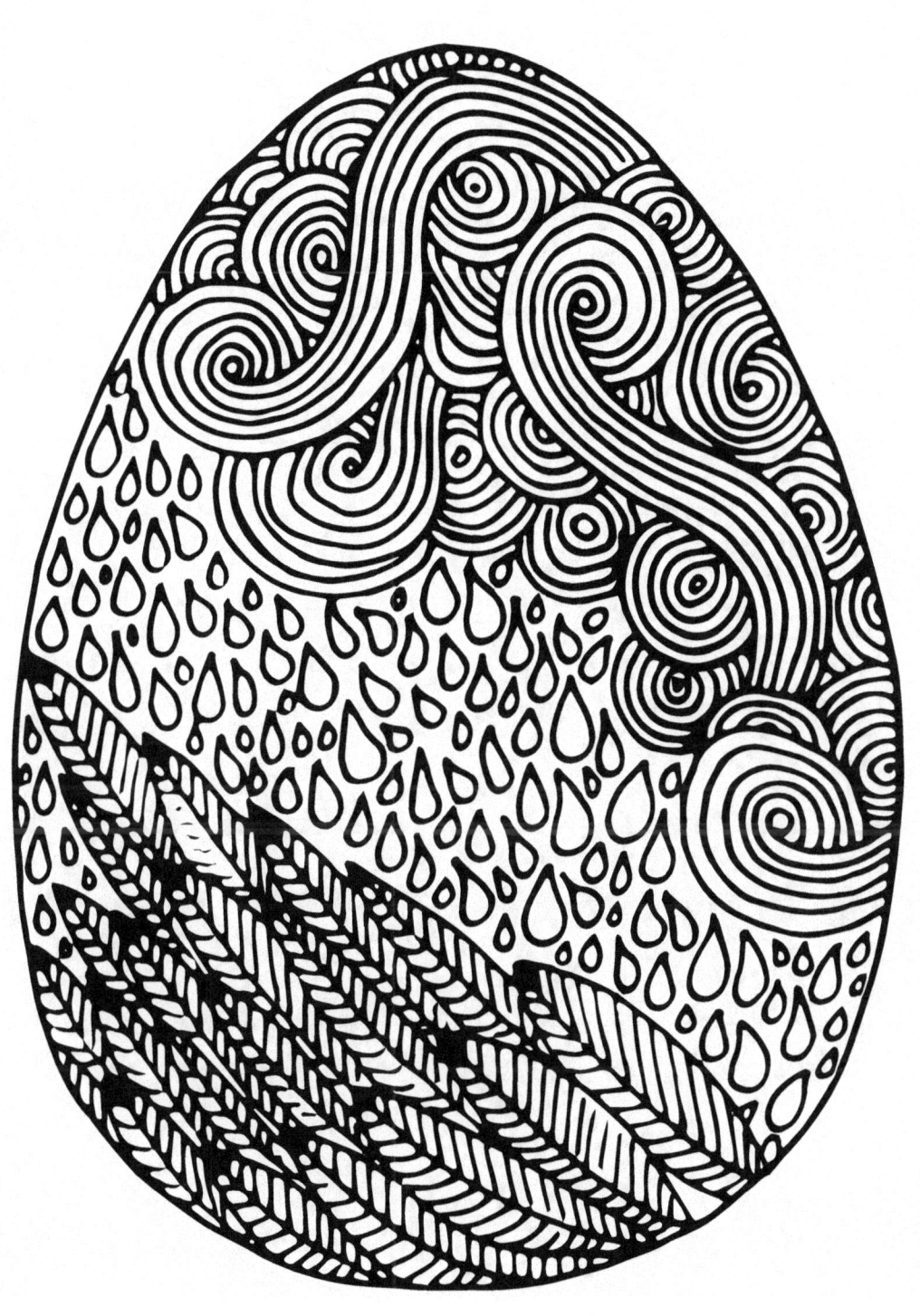

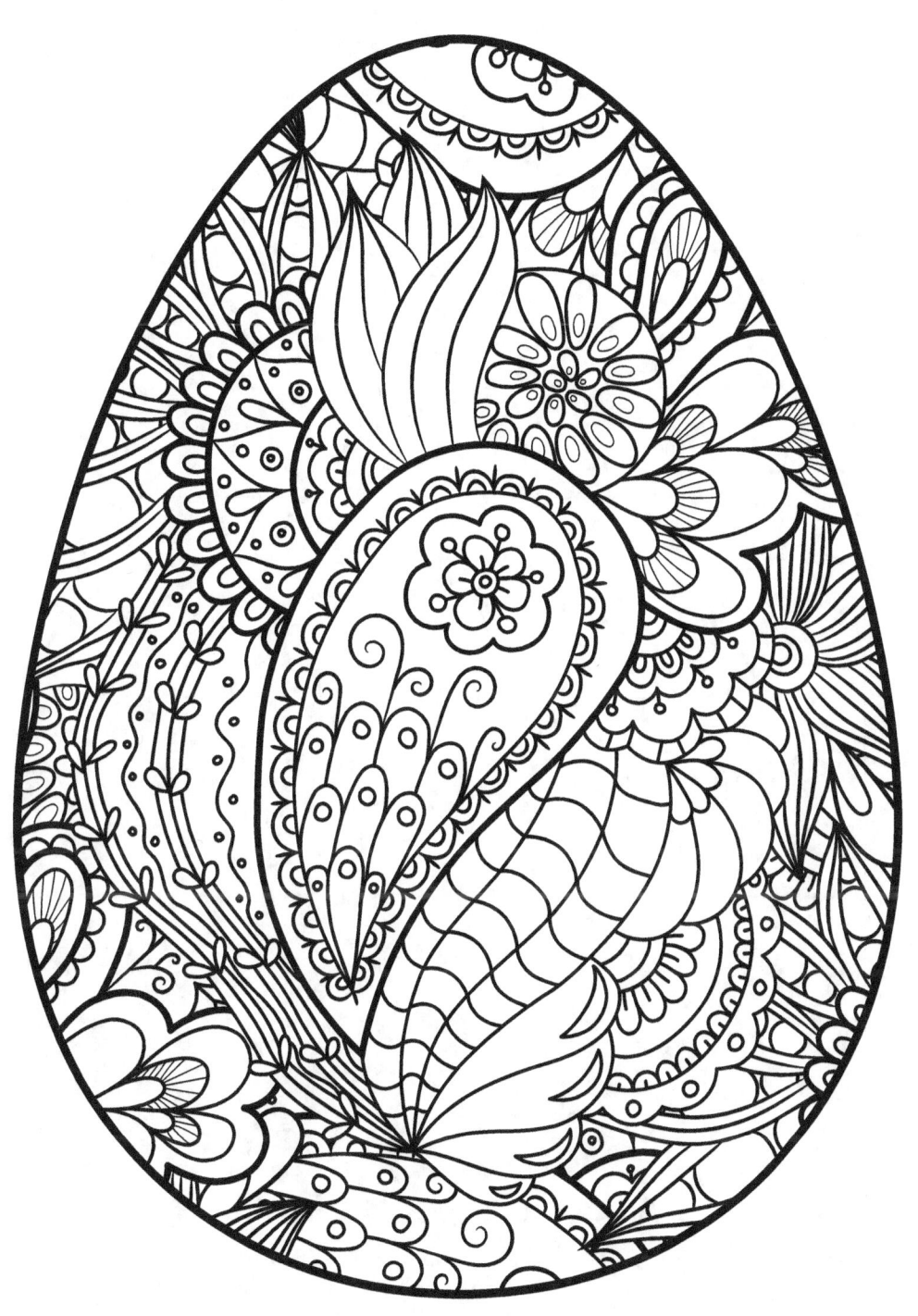

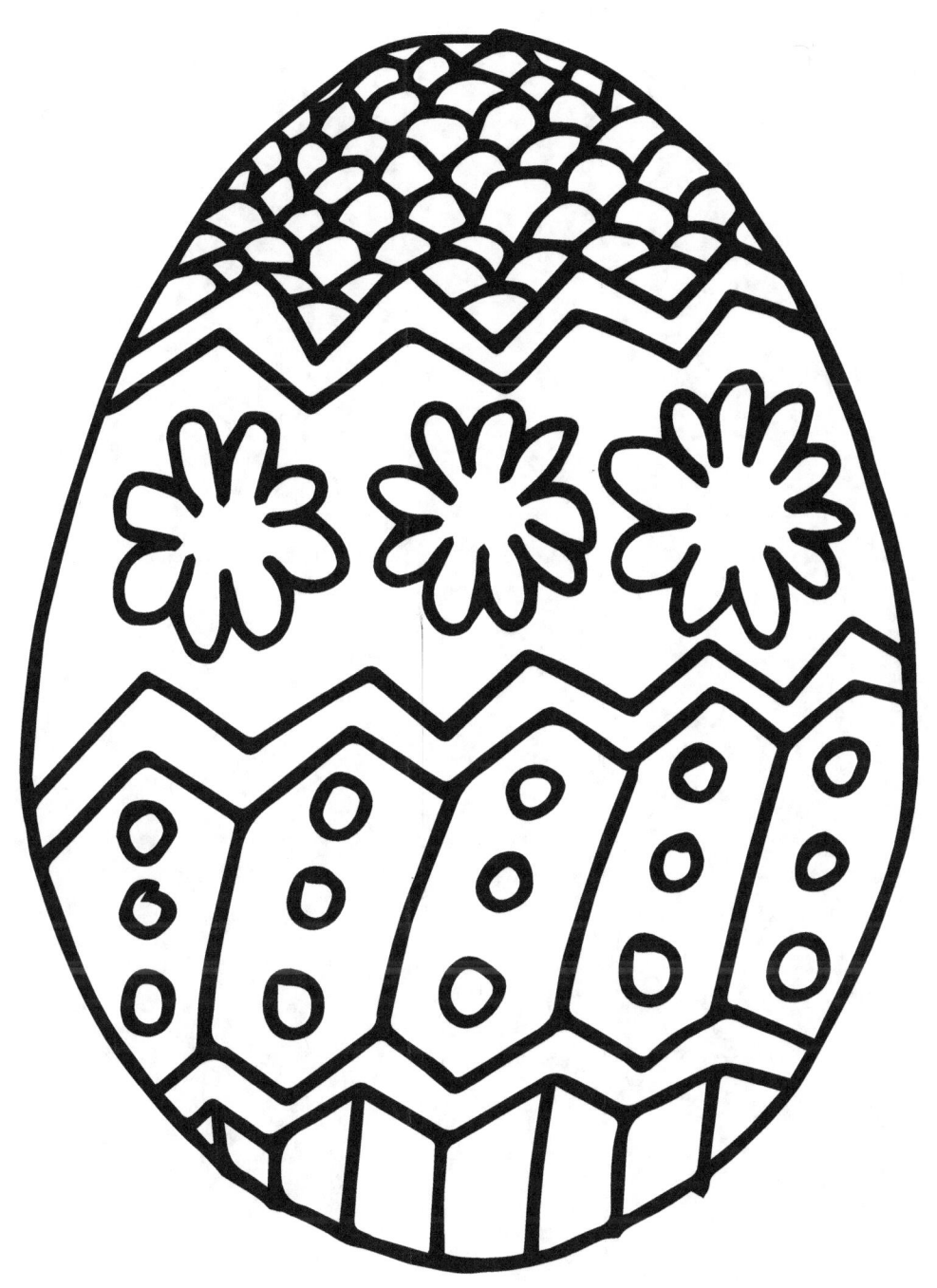

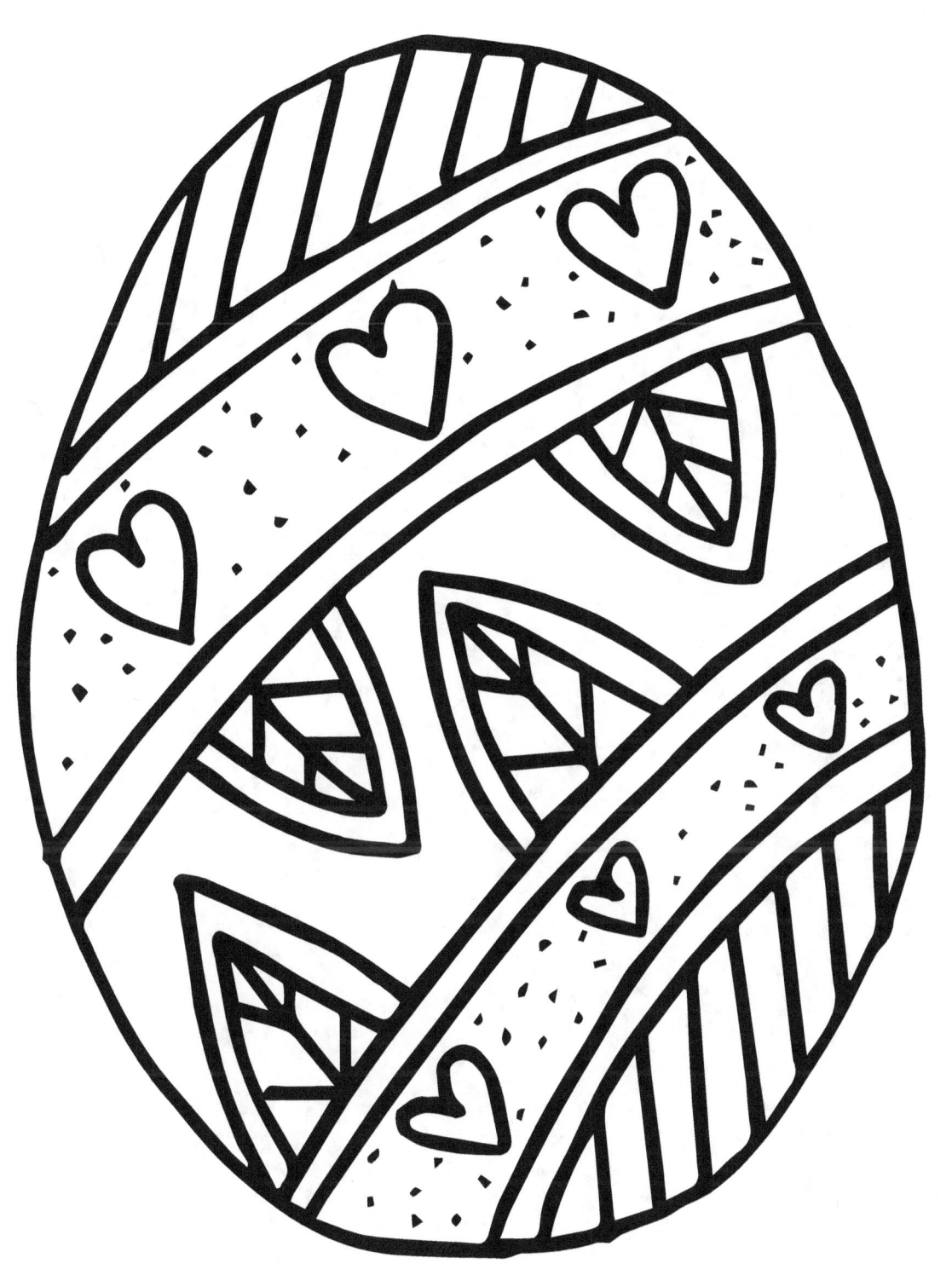

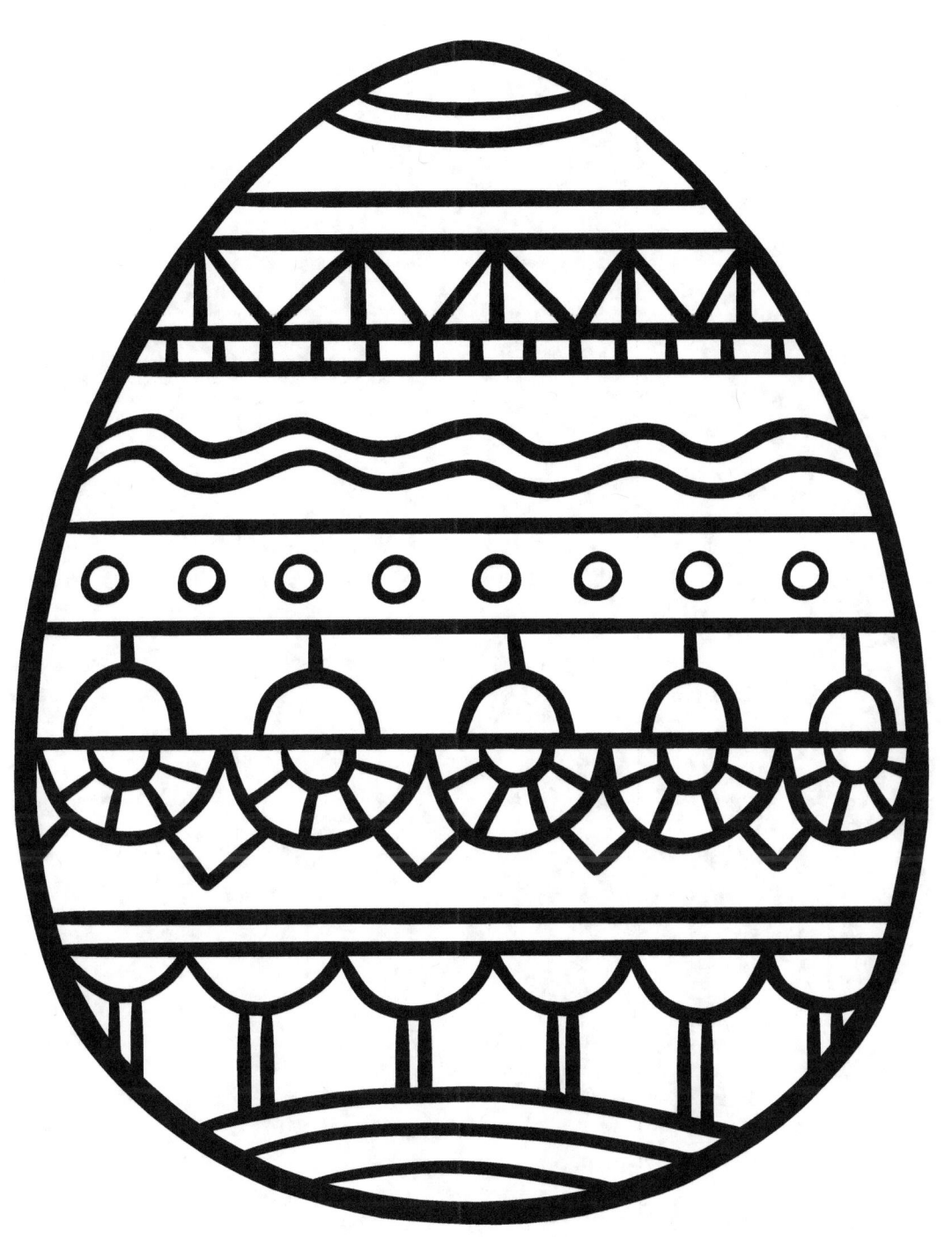

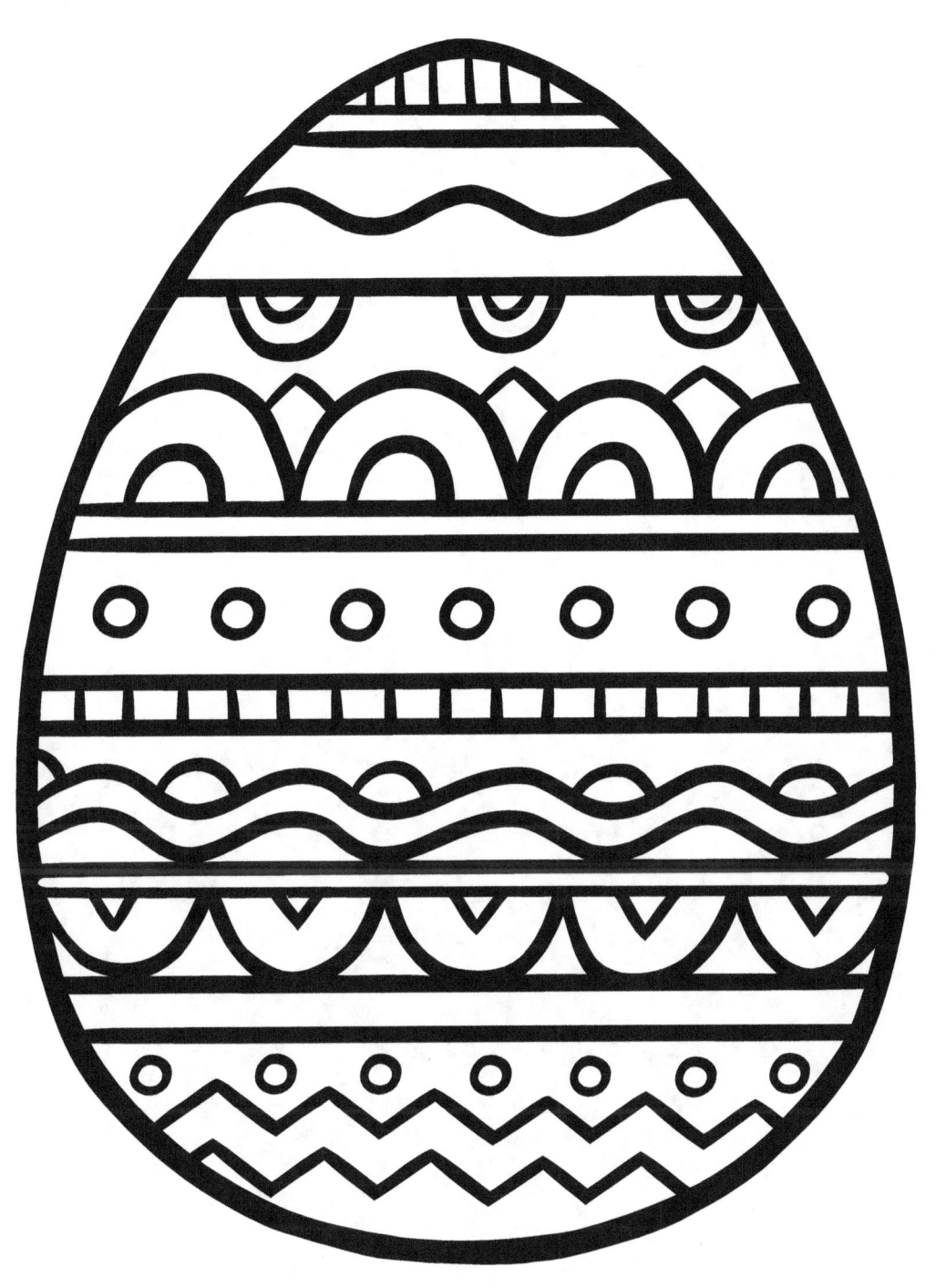

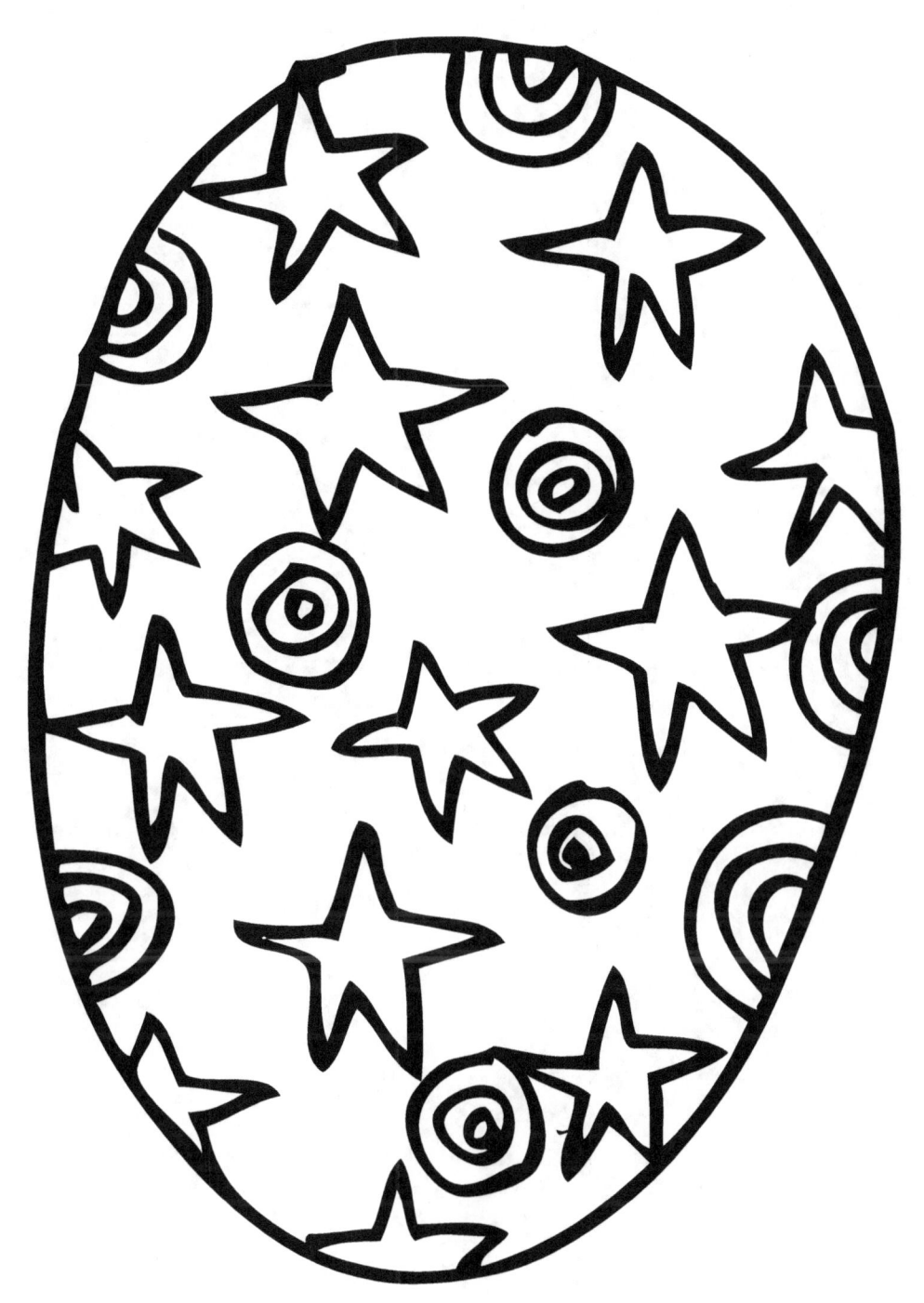

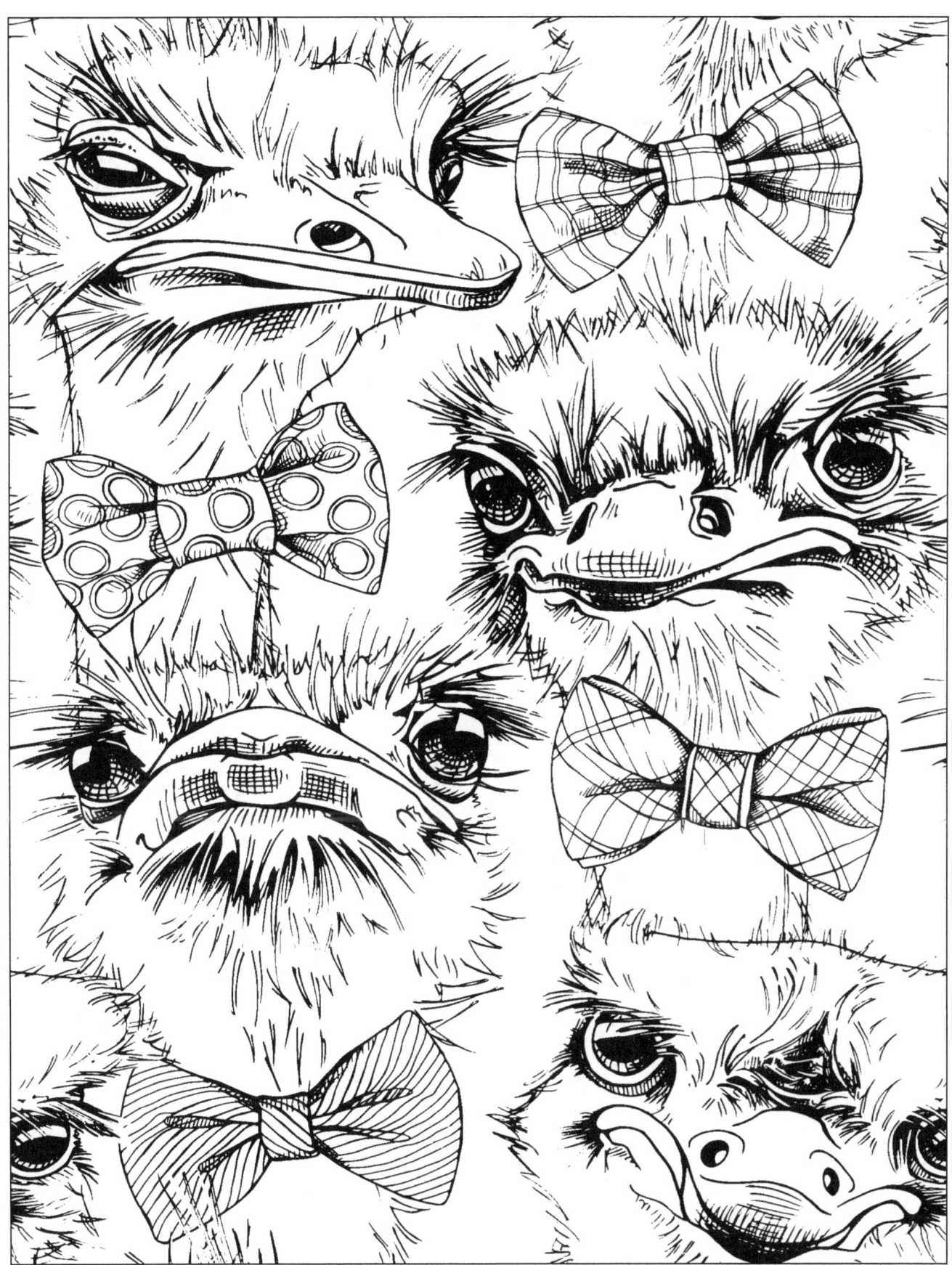

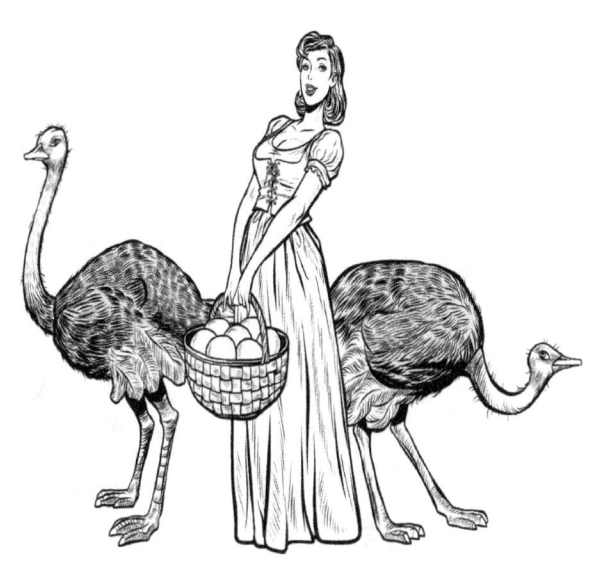

Thank you for your purchase

Please rate this book ☺

www.ingramcontent.com/pod-product-compliance
Lightning Source LLC
Chambersburg PA
CBHW082119220526
45472CB00009B/2241